REVELATION

MYSTERIUM SALUTIS

EDITED BY

JOHANNES FEINER
MAGNUS LÖHRER
THOMAS F. O'MEARA

REVELATION

HEINRICH FRIES

HERDER AND HERDER

1969
HERDER AND HERDER NEW YORK
232 Madison Avenue, New York, N.Y. 10016

Nihil obstat: Leo J. Steady, Censor Librorum
Imprimatur: ✠Robert F. Joyce, Bishop of Burlington
August 17, 1968

Library of Congress Catalog Card Number: 68–55085

CONTENTS

FOREWORD

What was previously a theological area prominent mainly for a detailed and static treatment in Latin volumes has become one of the leading problems of religious education and post-conciliar theology. *Revelation*, the theology of Christian historical and central revelation, is now seen as crucial for so many aspects of the Christian Gospel. At the same time, it has become clear that in our reflection now on God's revealing self-disclosure we find also the conjunctures of history, human mental structure, faith, society and world-view, and salvation history with Jesus Christ as its focal point. Karl Barth's theology of the Word of God, and Paul Tillich's synthesis of existential questions correlated with revelatory answering symbols, Rudolf Bultmann's demythologizing, and present existential eschatology are first theologies of revelation. Karl Rahner's most lasting contribution may be his affirmation and description of the divine milieu of grace open implicitly to the anonymous Christian; this is a new theology of revelation for less explicit and more searching times. *The Secular City* by Harvey Cox, J. Moltmann's *Theology of Hope*, the present and future oriented essays by Gabriel Moran go further: they are concerned with how revelation is not just a past event but a present experience experienced by the future. In the light of the past happenings begins promise for the future. A theology of social change and revolution soon arrives at the discovery that the Church has a responsibility neither to solve all the world's problems (which are too complex and too transitory) nor to ignore them, but rather to speak a Christian prophetic word.

7

This is derived as closely as possible from the sacramental and biblical gospel word.

In short, at every serious stage in the renewal of the Church and at the initiation of a more mature dialogue with our society we encounter the new problematic of revelation. It is no longer developed as a series of shocking disruptions of human history or as the pedagogic listing of revealed statements. Revelation is the presence in a human person, Jesus, living in his world and history of the self-disclosing Word of God. In his incarnation (*Logos*) is the culmination of the promise-filled Old Testament words (*dabar*) and the catalyst for the biblical words (good news). For the 1970's two problems assume prominence: (1) How can the personal history of Jesus of Nazareth and the only full access to that history, faith, be harmonized? (2) How can a unique personal and saving history which took place two thousand years ago be existentially and creatively present today and even move towards us in a coming parousia?

During the past decades Heinrich Fries has been a leading figure in the German ecumenical movement. His idea of "participation" by Protestant Churches in the ecclesial reality of Christianity had a marked influence at Vatican II. A pupil of J. Geiselmann and a former professor of fundamental theology at the University of Tübingen, he stands in the tradition of the Catholic Tübingen School where Johann Adam Möhler pioneered as open, dialogical theology ended the era of *Kontroverstheologie* as the form of Catholic-Protestant relationships. Dr. Fries wrote his dissertation on the thinkers and themes of the philosophy of religion in Germany between the wars; subsequent university work concentrated on Newman, whose complete works he is editing in German. He has written books on ecclesiology, on Bultmann and Barth, on contemporary philosophy and secularity. In the early 1960's he

8

left his professorship at Tübingen (his successor was Hans Küng) and joined the faculty at the University of Munich. While continuing his professorship, he developed the Institute for Ecumenical Research there.

The following pages are not an all-encompassing synthesis of revelation. Such a study is not yet possible, for the biblical problems are as vast as are the philosophical and social. What makes Fries's work valuable is that it competently presents two of the five important dimensions, the ecumenical and the biblical (the others being relationship to society, presence in today's thought forms, relationship to the future). Fries continues in terms of a biblical theology of both Testaments respecting the evolutionary and open character of the process. His approach throughout is ecumenical, and being a systematic (fundamental) theologian he concentrates on an exposition of three great dogmatic expositions of revelation from the Protestant and Catholic traditions in the twentieth century: Vatican I, dialectical theology, Vatican II. Vatican I's emphasis on the role of natural approach to God along with its limitations on science or reason as a replacement for the revelatory Word to Jews and Christians. The new beginnings made by dialectical theology came after the collapse of Hegelian optimism, romanticism, and political ineptitude in the holocaust of World War I. Karl Barth emphasized the otherness of God, the sovereignty of his Word to man's condition, and the unique saving power of God's Word. This saving Word was the commanding focus of belief, preaching, and theology. Rudolf Bultmann continued this verbal emphasis in his theology of biblical hermeneutics, form-criticism, and demythologizing. However, he located his hermeneutic not in God's revealing biblical word but in human existence. Fries considers the word-theology of Barth, Bultmann, and Emil Brunner. He contrasts their biblical theology with the concerns of the

Reformation, and their wrestling with the problems of God's actual "intervention" with the Roman Catholic theology of grace working within, through, and upon nature. Vatican II tested its ability to accept the theological currents of our century and to renew the Roman Catholic Church during its opening debates on revelation. Were the answers to the new questions to be from nineteenth-century essentialistic textbooks or were they to respect the issues of today and the biblical movement? As its courage to consider revelation openly went, so went the Council itself. Success produced one of the finest documents of Vatican II. It describes revelation as an interplay of deeds and words; it makes the Bible central above the Church; it admits that tradition is active in the Church's making revelation present but in a different way (especially as to content) than Scripture; it gives place to the entire Church to be active in interpretation, authority, and tradition without eliminating either charism or office.

Fries balances his systematic study of revelation with a biblical theology of both Testaments. He brings together the evolutionary and open character of the process present in Judaeo-Christian salvation history and the broader dimensions of primitive and world religious history. "Natural theology" is described in terms of creation and of a general salvation history. The latter recognizes the role of grace and grace's spark of implicit revelation in all human religions (Rahner, Tillich). The presence of Christ-merited grace is more pervasive than the power of rational theodicy. So God's presence in man and in cosmos and his Christocentric grace lie behind the world religions and general salvation history. Fries develops his biblical theology from two points of view: promise and fulfillment. The first corresponds to the Old Testament; the second includes the New Testament but goes beyond it. Continuing the framework of a dynamic process, he emphasizes in conclusion the eschatological realization of Christ's past earthly life for us now as we are caught up in various planes of forward evolution, and for the future kingdom of God coming towards us.

THOMAS F. O'MEARA

REVELATION

INTRODUCTION

There is a definite connection between revelation and salvation history because both refer to the same thing, though from different points of view. Thus we might say that revelation is present to the world in salvation history, and that, on the other hand, salvation history can be defined as man's historical encounter with revelation. Seen in this light, revelation and salvation history are frames of reference which, each in its own way, comprise all that is or can be called the object of theology or of Christian faith. Thus, further, they can both be called transcendental frames of theological reference, insofar as they connote in themselves the underlying basis and the subject and content of all of the various branches of theological science. As such frames of reference they help us to understand all the many details of Christianity, for they relate the theological parts to the theological whole.

The attempt to situate theology within such a transcendental frame of reference is a distinct preoccupation of modern times and is a reflection of the transcendental philosophical method which has so dominated contemporary theological thought. Following philosophy, theology is inescapably faced with inquiring into its very basis, into the conditions under which it is possible. Since this inquiry attempts to deal comprehensively with fundamental principles, it is therefore also possible to view revelation and salvation history as fundamental theology, with fundamental theology being defined as an inquiry into the very basis of theological science.

se, theology's inquiry into its underlying principles
something new. Such philosophical schools as deism,
sm, idealism, positivism, and materialism, among others,
reviously required theology to test its ground. Yet today
lestion of theological conditions has been narrowed down
to at of whether revelation is at all possible—and also appropriate, and even whether it is necessary. Inevitably, the norma-
tive transcendental theological concept has therefore been
that of revelation.

Strictly speaking, the concept of revelation is more comprehensive than that of salvation history. It is wider ranging, less
restricted, and more formal; it includes not only the history
of salvation—and history in general—but also all other possible
ways of revelation. Yet the concept of salvation history is
probably no less transcendental, for otherwise it could not be
used as the basic concept and theological principle of the work
at hand. But to use the idea of salvation history in such a way
requires that what is implicit in it, and what is assumed as the
necessary condition under which it is possible, be made explicit.

One final note in this regard: the coordination of revelation
and salvation history is faced also with the problem and phenomenon of history. History lies at the heart of contemporary
philosophical thought, and a living theology must take account
of it. History and historicity—together with man's realization
and language of his existential situation—have thus become
basic theological questions. Specifically, they have raised the
question of revelation as history.

As a transcendental theological concept, revelation has also
been viewed in another context, especially within Protestant
theology, namely, as the word of God. The word of God is
taken to be a fundamental and comprehensive description of
the object of faith and the content of theology. There is no
doubt that this definition is possible, once we explain what the
word of God signifies, what it assumes, what it includes in its

16

content, fulfillment, and utterance, and what its consequences are.

Yet here again revelation possesses a greater width and scope than even the word, for the word is uttered within the framework of revelation. On the other hand, revelation is articulated and made specific through the word of God, just as it is through history as salvation history.

All of the above goes to show that revelation is not merely a possible transcendental theological concept, but a necessary one on account of its comprehensive scope. It is the fundamental principle of theology and faith.

I. THE CATHOLIC CONCEPT OF REVELATION

A. The Catholic Understanding of Revelation after Vatican I

We noted in our Introduction that, as a result of contemporary philosophical investigation, revelation is presently being treated as an inclusive, transcendental theological term, and that the question of the possibility and conditions of theology has thus become the question of the possibility and reality of revelation. This question has in fact preoccupied the modern Church, and was the special and explicit concern of the First Vatican Council. In contrast to earlier councils—including the Council of Trent—Vatican I pronounced upon questions involving the principles underlying, embracing, and at the same time transcending the whole content of faith and revelation. Thus it can be described as a council concerned with the problems of fundamental theology. The theme of this first council of the Vatican indicated that it was concerned with the issues of its own time, and that it saw itself obliged to deliberate and decide for its own time, and to react against the errors of its own time (summarized some years previously in the "Syllabus of Errors").

Vatican I's *Constitution on Catholic Faith* gives a definition of revelation which seeks to develop the Catholic understanding of revelation against any attack upon its possibility, reality, or meaningfulness, its intelligibility or legitimacy, and also against any attempt to diminish it or to interpret it in an immanentist or psychologistic direction. The decisive text reads:

> The same holy Mother Church holds and teaches that God, the origin and end of all things, can be known with certainty by the natural light of human reason from the things that he created; "for since the creation of the world his invisible attributes are clearly seen, being understood through the things that are made" (Romans 1, 20); and she teaches that it was nevertheless the good pleasure of his wisdom and goodness to reveal himself and the eternal decrees of his will to the human race in another and supernatural way, as the Apostle says: "God, who at sundry times and in divers manners spoke in times past to the fathers by the prophets, last of all in these days has spoken to us by his Son" (Hebrews 1, 1 f.).[1]

Pronouncements of the magisterium such as these give no description of revelation, no explanation of the concept, no definition. They use the Latin word *"revelare,"* and since this word is not more fully explained in such texts, it is permissible to study its original meaning. *Re-velare* is quite specific in concept: it means to take away the *velum*, or veil, or cover. It means to make known, to reveal openly; what was previously covered and invisible is now "lifted up" into sight. When *revelare* is predicated of God, it assumes that God is a hidden God; the meaning is that God's concealment and invisibility are unveiled and manifested. For in the act of revealing, some thing or some one is always made manifest. Thus revelation includes two things in one: the act and faculty of revealing, and what is revealed in this act.

The conciliar text cited above also makes it possible for us to speak of different forms and modes of revelation. For the words of the council say that God determined to manifest the

---

[1] J. Neuner and H. Roos, *Der Glaube der Kirche in den Urkunden der Lehrverkündigung* (Regensburg, 1958), pp. 31 f.

decrees of his will "in another and supernatural way," thus implying and presupposing that a first kind of revelation has taken place. Now if this last form of revelation is called supernatural, then the first can only be natural, even though it is not expressly so called. In the words of the council, natural revelation took place and is present in the work of creation, in creatures, in the creation of the world. Natural revelation makes it possible for us to see God as the source and goal of all things. The classic text for this view is contained in the Epistle to the Romans: "Ever since the creation of the world his invisible nature, namely, his eternal power and deity, has been clearly perceived in the things that have been made" (1, 20). This revelation of God is accessible to the natural light of reason, and accessible in the form of knowledge.

Nothing is said about how this knowledge is imparted, nor about how many men possess it. But a very important clause in the conciliar text makes a clear statement about the concrete realization of this knowledge of God. Revelation in the supernatural sense derives its necessary function and significance from the fact that aspects of God not in themselves accessible to human reason cannot be known easily, with firm certainty, and without admixture of error by everyone under the present conditions of the human race.

In order that we may understand the definitions of the council with regard to natural revelation and its knowledge of God, we must view both ways together. The result is not a contradictory or dialectical statement but a description of the whole situation. In each case, in different terms, we have a description of the limits of what is really possible, and the actual degree to which the limits are or are not being reached and attained in concrete historical fact. The council describes what men have or have not succeeded in making of this possibility. Thus it unites the abstract and metaphysical point of view with the concrete view of the history of salvation.

21

Furthermore, these definitions are analogous to the double structure of the statements contained in the Epistle to the Romans, which includes not only a clearly formulated assertion of the knowledge of God, but also one of human guilt: the wrath of God is revealed from heaven against men "who by their wickedness suppress the truth" (1, 18); "for although they knew God they did not honor him as God or give thanks to him, but they became futile in their thinking and their senseless minds were darkened" (1, 21).

When theology, following these texts from Scripture and the magisterium, speaks of the "natural revelation" of God, it is offering what is referred to in dogmatic statements and in the Bible as a revelation in creation and through creation, in and through the works of God. Creation and nature, concepts which we customarily associate with one another, in no way come from the same roots and origin. Nature, φύσις, is a concept of Greek philosophy, and does not at all imply the creation by God from nothing; it even implies the contrary, what has come into being from itself. On the other hand, creation, *creatura*, is a theological concept which explicitly opposes the idea that nature has come into being from itself, and replaces φύσις by κτίσις, nature by the creation. But it is possible and legitimate (and this shows how much concepts can change meaning) to integrate nature into creation, and thus to separate the concept of nature from its origins and understand it as creation. This is the meaning of "nature" and "natural" in the theological expression "natural revelation." It is the revelation of God in the creation, the revelation of God in his words.

To sum up: natural revelation means in objective terms the creation—and principally and essentially man, its highest achievement—insofar as, on the basis of created being and the similarity to the being of the creator which this basis implies (as we say: on the basis of the analogy of being), it makes known and manifests the existence and nature of God

22

who is above and beyond the world. But this is done insofar as man can apprehend, perceive, know, and understand this manifestation by the light of his natural reason and can express it in words—for the revelation which is present and manifests itself in created being is also brought to light through the word. Consequently, man as a creature endowed with intellect is a revelation of God to a degree infinitely greater than the rest of creation: man is created "in God's image and likeness" and displays the dignity which is his through the domination which he exercises over the creation by the use of his intellect and word (see Genesis 1, 26 f.).

Supernatural revelation, as distinguished from "natural revelation," is that form of the unveiling of God which, objectively, is not given in creation or in man, and which subjectively cannot be acquired by the unaided understanding of the human mind. Let us try to define this form of revelation more precisely.

Supernatural revelation transcends the revelation given in nature as the work and creation of God. It consists in God's manifesting "himself and his will" in a way which cannot be inferred or presumed on the basis of creation and man. The basic form of this manifestation is the person; the basic form of the self-revelation takes place in the word by contrast to revelation in the work of creation. But the word which is uttered in this supernatural revelation—by contrast to the word of man, who can know of God, and therefore can also speak of God (thus possessing a natural word of God)—must be characterized as the word and utterance of God himself, as the Word of God which can never be discovered by any human word about God.

This word has been uttered in two ways, according to the pattern laid down in the Epistle to the Hebrews (1, 1): ". . . of old to our fathers by the prophets" and the bearers of divine messages, decrees, and commands; and to us "in these last days," the present time, in the Son, who is the Word of God in person. Revelation in word culminates in revelation in person. But it remains revelation in the word, because the Son is the Word.

Supernatural revelation took place in history at particular periods and moments, in the past and in the present. This means that it has taken concrete form in a particular time and place, at a particular point within the world. Natural revelation came at the beginning of history, insofar as "history" began with creation. At any point within what was there begun, within the course of history as a whole, natural revelation was in principle open to all men everywhere and in every age; it is a general revelation. Nevertheless, supernatural revelation transmitted through the prophets and the Son, and by that fact a special revelation, was also intended for all men, for the whole human race.

Supernatural revelation is encountered by man not merely in the form of some object existing "in itself," something outside him; deep within him it concerns and affects him profoundly. It reveals to him something decisive about himself; it shows him that he is destined to have personal fellowship with God who is revealing himself in word and person, in wisdom and love. The aim and destiny of man is God. If by his origin and existential life man is called to a supernatural goal which transcends him, if man infinitely surpasses man (as Pascal has said), and if God alone ultimately and exclusively satisfies the human spirit and the human heart, then supernatural revelation, in the form of the personal self-manifestation of God and the revealing of his eternal decrees of salvation, is necessary for the sake of this ultimate aim and destiny of man, and for the meaning it gives to human existence. Supernatural revelation was absolutely necessary, said Vatican I, "because God, out of his infinite goodness, destined man to a supernatural end, that is, to a participation in the good things of God, which altogether exceed human understanding; for 'eye has not seen nor ear heard, nor has it entered into the heart of man, what things God has prepared for those who love him' (1 Corinthians 2, 9)."

This passage shows how supernatural revelation is strictly orientated towards man; its meaning and significance are both directly relevant to his life [*existentiell*] and provide the ultimate interpretation of his existence [*existential*]. It is also clear that the way in which man is constituted includes this supernatural element determining the nature of his existence, and also the natural desire of seeing God. Man is "nature," called to be supernatural; he comes to be himself through the truth and the coming about of this revelation, in the sense that he thereby attains the highest realization and fulfillment of his own proper being. This shows that it is an offense against his existential being, and therefore unnatural for him to shut himself off from the supernatural in this sense, and to reject it.

Supernatural revelation as the word, the fact, and the event of God imparting himself cannot be derived from man nor deduced from the natural revelation; that is why it is called supernatural. It can be received, heard, and understood only as something wholly new, coming from God's free love, bestowed by his mercy and grace without any obligation on his part.

Of course, as a person endowed with intellect, man is by nature open without limitation to everything that exists; he is a "hearer of the word" in the widest and most universal sense, and is capable of speaking truly but in human terms about God. But it is not possible to deduce from this fact the certainty of a spontaneous and loving self-revelation of God to man (for God might be and remain a silent God). This new revelation of God can be perceived through the fact that man does not merely listen to the word he himself utters, but believes, in the sense of the expressions "I believe you," "I believe in you." In faith, the believer is lifted up into fellowship with God who reveals himself; he bases himself upon God, and participates in the being, knowledge, word, wisdom, and love of God, whom he believes. In faith, supernatural reality is disclosed to man, while at the same time he is given the ability to hear and understand it.

However right and necessary it is, for the sake of a clear understanding and an awareness of the differences between natural and supernatural revelation, to distinguish one from the other and to characterize them as general and special revelation, it is equally necessary to appreciate the connection between the two forms of revelation. It is the one God who reveals himself in creation, and at the same time in word, act, history; and in its personal, human form it is one and the same man to whom revelation is given and towards whom it is directed as knowledge and as faith.

Revelation in creation, in the work of God, and in man, is the prerequisite for the revelation of God in his acts, word, history, and person. The well-known scholastic axiom expresses this in a phrase: grace presupposes nature. The prerequisites for supernatural revelation are the world, creation, and above all man in his humanity as a person endowed with intellect, man the hearer of the word, an historical free being capable of transcending himself and yet created. Supernatural revelation makes use of language and other means of expression provided in creation. On the other hand, the natural is integrated into the supernatural and is in fact brought to its ultimate perfection: *gratia perficit et complet naturam*. Revelation in creation is taken up into the revelation in word and person and given its own proper value; it is consummated in the form of a new creation, a new life, a rebirth.

In another expression which has obtained wide currency, Karl Barth describes creation as the outward basis of the covenant, and the covenant as the inner substance of creation.

The final goal and the ultimate consummation of man is to have fellowship with God, to partake of the goodness of God, to "see him as he is" (1 John 3, 2), to "understand fully, even as [we] have been fully understood" (1 Corinthians 13, 12).

However, what we have said must not be taken to mean that supernatural revelation represents an uninterrupted process in the perfection of man and human nature. For man in his concrete, historical existence is fallen nature. The perverse tendencies of nature, insofar as it is fallen, cannot be brought to perfection; the self-will of sinful man must first be broken, before he can attain to his true perfection. Thus man must be converted and "lose himself," and so truly find himself: he must "deny himself." Consequently, the grace of God towards fallen nature is the "grace of the cross," which was vouchsafed through the self-emptying of God in the obedience unto death of Jesus Christ.

The theological basis, the reason which follows from the nature of God for this close coordination between the natural and the supernatural, is provided by the fact that—to use Johannine language (John 1, 1 ff.)—in the beginning there was the Word (*logos*), the Word which was with God, and which was God himself; everything exists through the Word and nothing was made without the Word; this Word became flesh and lived among us. The same fact is expressed in the language of the Pauline captivity epistles, where we read that Christ is the "first-born of all creation," that in him all things were created, in heaven and on earth, visible and invisible, that all things were created through him and for him, and that in him all things hold together (Colossians 1, 15 ff.).

Similarly, the Pauline conception of the new Adam and the new man underlies this inner relationship, and is a background to the statement, "For it is the God who said, 'Let light shine out of darkness,' who has shone in our hearts to give the light of the knowledge of the glory of God in the face of Christ" (2 Corinthians 4, 6).

Finally, the relationship between the two modes of revelation is apparent from the inner significance of both. Revelation through the works which God has made is also a revelation through the word. The creation came into being through the word (John 1, 3). It is God's will to say something in his works: "The heavens are telling the glory of God" (Psalm 19, 1). But man, as a creature endowed with intellect and capable of uttering the word, is the middle point in which this exchange between God's work and word takes place.

Revelation in the word is also a revelation in God's works, in deeds and facts, for it takes place within history. It is God's will to speak, to utter his own proper word, in the history of the people of Israel, in Israel's election, vocation, salvation, and affliction, in covenant; this continues in the events to which the New Testament bears witness: in the incarnation, in what took place in Jesus, in what Jesus did (Acts 1, 1), and above all in Jesus' cross and exaltation.

B. The Catholic Concept of Revelation as a Problem for Ecumenical Theology

If revelation is a fundamental and a transcendental theological concept, it is to be expected that it would be an object of theological dialogue between different Christian communities, and that it too would manifest theological and denominational differences. The differences concern the distinction between natural and supernatural revelation, and also the understanding of revelation in general.

The origin of this different understanding of revelation can be found in the basic principles of Protestant theology. For Luther, the distinction between *theologia gloriae* and *theologia crucis* was one of the fundamental concerns of his theological purpose and understanding. By *theologia gloriae*, Luther meant a natural knowledge of God, the knowledge of God's power and glory obtained from the creation, from his "works." Here Luther had the statements of the Epistle to the Romans (1, 18. 32) expressly in mind, and interpreted them to mean that the Apostle was calling those men fools who were concerned with knowledge of this kind. Luther contrasts this kind of knowledge and person with genuine theology and the true theologian. As early as the Heidelberg Disputation of 1518 he stated, "He is rightly called a theologian who understands as much of God's being as is visible and turned towards the world, as it is presented in the passion and the cross." It is utterances such as these which underlie the *theologia crucis*. This is theology in the true sense, because it does not seek to know God according to the powers given to man and with the help of analogical thinking, but is orientated exclusively towards the "deity of God" and his revelation in Jesus Christ. Humility, suffering, shame, and the cross—these are completely opposed to inadequate human pictures and conceptions of God. Here the concealment of God is revealed. This does not refer to the—invisible—being and nature of God, but is meant to describe the action of God in Jesus Christ, the event of Christ, which became visible in the world concealed under its contrary and in paradox. This concealment of God under his contrary is what Paul calls the "folly of the cross," which at the same time is the wisdom of God; it puts to shame the wisdom of men (1 Corinthians 1, 18 ff.) Luther asserts, then, that true theology and the true knowledge of God is to be found only in Christ crucified.

This distinction between *theologia gloriae* and *theologia crucis* does away with the terminology of "natural and supernatural revelation," although what this terminology refers to remains; but the truth and theological meaningfulness of the *theologia gloriae*—the natural revelation and the knowledge of God based upon it—are denied. Consequently, it is impossible to bring it into any positive coordination with the *theologia crucis*. All analogies are dissolved for the sake of "Christ alone," the "cross alone."

Catholic theology in dialogue with these problems posed by Luther's theology of the cross, first asks whether this unquestionably profound conception of revelation is capable of expressing everything which the testimony of the Scripture requires to be said, particularly with regard to the person and works of Jesus Christ in the context of salvation history. We must ask whether the ultimate revelation in Jesus Christ, and in him crucified, permits the exclusive consequences which Luther draws from it. Finally, does this theological conception preserve the truth that man is both a creature and the image of God, that man has a basic reference towards God from which it is possible to attain true knowledge? Is this truth indispensable, even before the *theologia crucis?*

As it is presented in the Epistle to the Romans, the "folly" of men does not consist in their attempt to know the eternal power and deity of God from the creation, but in the fact that they have dishonored, perverted, and falsified the "truth" revealed in creation. The *theologia crucis* is not opposed to the knowledge of God from the works of the creation, which possesses the quality of revelation, but to a *gnosis* which despises the cross, to man's endeavor not to acknowledge the truth given him from creation. This leads to conclusions different from Luther's concerning the relationship between *theologia gloriae* and *theologia crucis*.

The distinction between natural and supernatural revelation and its delineation in the Catholic understanding of revelation has repeatedly been attacked in modern Protestant theology, especially by Emil Brunner and Karl Barth. Until now it has been supposed as possible and necessary to advance this issue as the specific point characterizing the Protestant objection to Catholic belief. In answering this objection, Catholic theology has endeavored to present a better and clearer picture of the way in which it understands its own nature and its own teaching.

Referring to the definitions of Vatican I, Brunner states that according to the Catholic view, reason is wholly and completely adequate to deal with "nature," while only the "supernatural," that which concerns redemption, is the province of faith: "Here is nature, there is grace, here is reason, there is revelation, both distinct from one another like the first and second storeys of a house, neatly separated by a horizontal line." According to this view, Catholic theology presents a self-contained, self-subsistent, and self-sufficient system of reason and nature. In contrast to it, says Brunner, the Protestant understanding of nature speaks of creation only through faith, of nature as creation; it speaks in theological terms and in its total context, and recognizes creation only as a fallen creation, a "shattered mirror," it has to describe man as "man in revolt." For Barth, even this conception put forward by Brunner recognizing in the fact of human responsibility some remnant of the image of God in man and some point of contact for revelation, was still too positive. Barth regards human nature as a radical, sinful refusal of revelation. His formula "God is hidden, man is blind" gives an accurate picture of his view. Consequently, for Barth, revelation is a new creation carried out without any prerequisite whatsoever; it is identical with atonement.

Only through misunderstanding can the Catholic concept of natural revelation be interpreted to mean that nature is an autonomous self-contained reality which can be fathomed and understood by reason, that it is like the first storey of a building, an apartment equipped with every convenience, on top of which the superstructure of grace and supernatural can be built. This misunderstanding sees the abstract ancillary concept of pure nature (which, since the controversy with Baius, theology has envisaged as a possibility, making use of it as a kind of static "constructional formula" [Hans Urs von Balthasar] in order to clarify the free and incalculable character of grace yet at the same time pointing out it has never in fact existed) and equates it with the concept of nature, which denotes the concrete reality of creation as determined by salvation history. But it is only the latter concept of nature which the Catholic faith refers to when it speaks of natural revelation. This concept contains an explicit denial of what Brunner asserts, that nature is separate, self-contained, self-sufficient, and isolated from the supernatural.

In addition, Catholic understanding of supernatural revelation is often characterized by present-day Protestant theology as an intellectualist and rationalist conception. This view is the expression of a further disagreement. According to Brunner, Catholicism regards revelation as the disclosing of new truths concerning God, an increase in our knowledge of God, which without revelation would be closed and shut off from us. Brunner characterizes the Catholic conception of revelation by saying that it always concerns an object, a "something," a doctrine. Accordingly, Catholic belief is belief in an object, a "something." In Brunner's view this has the ominous and dangerous consequence that faith, which represents a personal encounter between two subjects, between God and man, is turned into a neutral and impersonal attitude to facts, a doctrinal belief. He adds, "This change in the understanding of faith, which turned a relationship of trust and obedience with the Lord of the Church into an authoritarian biblical and doctrinal belief, is the profoundest reason for the transformation and weakness of Christianity and the Church from the secondary century up to the present day."[2]

According to Brunner, the most serious consequence of this view, in which revelation becomes a doctrine, a truth, an idea, an object, consists in the fact that it reverses the true relationship between God and man. "So long as we are 'dealing with something' we are in control." Knowledge has its object at its disposal, and treats it as a thing to be mastered. This view maintain's man's autonomy and self-sufficient personal will; it offends against the basic relationship between God and man, which is essentially one in which "we are not in control, and where it is not we who are masters, but where God alone is Lord: *Tu solus Dominus.*"

Has Brunner rightly described the Catholic conception of supernatural revelation? In the first place, it must be admitted that many textbook accounts of revelation do indeed give this impression. Let us quote only one example. Revelation, according to one such text, "consists of the verbal imparting to men of those truths which serve towards the knowledge and attainment of his supernatural goal. Thus while natural revelation takes place through the act of creation itself and possesses its means of expression in the work of creation, supernatural revelation requires a further activity on the part of the divine omnipotence towards the human mind, endowed with reason, and teaches in a higher way through the forms of human speech."[3]

Apologetics texts on the whole give the impression that supernatural revelation is exclusively concerned with knowledge, that it provides an increase, extension, and enrichment of what we know, superimposed upon a basis of truths which can be known naturally. In association with this definition, the theological concept "mystery" is almost exclusively under-

---

[2] *Revelation and Reason* (Philadelphia, 1946).
[3] J. Brunsmann, *Lehrbuch der Apologetik,* I (Vienna, 1930), p. 147.

stood as distinct from reason: a mystery is what is not known or cannot be known.

But if there is to be any revelation of God to man, it must be possible for it to be apprehended by the mind of man. Therefore, the possibility of apprehension, intelligibility, and truth in the ontological sense is assumed. Within this framework, and on the basis of these assumptions, there can be a knowledge of revelation, a knowledge which partakes of the quality of truth. Brunner's specific question is whether, by receiving revelation in the form of truth and knowledge, we become masters of what we know. It is possibly to argue in this way only in terms of a particular view of knowledge where the subject controls the object, where the categories, the formative powers which give order to what lies outside the subjective realm and make it the object of knowledge, belong to the subject alone. On the basis of such a conception, which is drawn from the model of mathematics and natural science, it is understandable that in every case where knowledge is involved, the autonomous and controlling function of man comes into operation. It is also clear that an objection must be raised as far as the knowledge of God is concerned; for as Brunner points out, this implies an attempt to make God an object and so to control him.

But we can in fact say that the epistemological model assumed here does not represent the real structure. Knowledge does not mean to master and control data, but to accept and receive them. Man is a finite, questioning, receptive, and passive mind, dependent in the process of knowledge upon the outside world. The being towards which man reaches out beyond himself in knowledge is richer and more comprehensive than the objects which he knows at any time. This characteristic of human knowledge perceiving, accepting, encountering, is particularly manifest in the case of knowledge of another person—over whom no control is possible. It is realized to the

34

ultimate degree (and necessarily so realized) in the knowledge of the absolute and transcendent person of God.

In its own way, Vatican I took account of this fact: "If anyone says that a man cannot be lifted up by God to a knowledge and perfection which surpasses what is natural, but can and must ultimately attain of himself, in an uninterrupted progress, to the possession of all truth and goodness, let him be anathema."

With regard to the view that the Catholic conception of revelation is intellectualist, it can be said that this charge cannot be maintained if we consider the precise meaning of Vatican I, where following therefrom we need not arrive at either a one-sided intellectualist understanding of revelation, nor at the reduction of revelation's faith to a thing, but at the very view which underlies these objections.

The "other" supernatural way is described as follows: "It pleased the wisdom and love of God to reveal himself and the external decrees of his will to the human race." The unmistakable meaning of this statement is that in supernatural revelation God did not reveal a doctrine or an idea, but himself. The word "himself" is not qualified, and expresses with unmistakable force what Brunner, as well as almost every representative of Protestant theology, has found it necessary to assert (hitherto, principally in opposition to the Catholic view): *in revelation, God makes himself known, and imparts himself*. God discloses himself in the way in which it pleases his wisdom and loving kindness.

The revelation of Jesus Christ is the principal and supreme form of the self-revelation of God. Thus revelation is concerned not with a thing, but with a person. But if this is the case, then the encounter with this revelation cannot be an impersonal relationship, but is a personal encounter, such as is found in faith. Here the content and object of faith is not excluded, but included and affirmed. The basis for a faith

35

centering in statements is found in a faith grounded in an encounter, faith in a "thou," in another person directly encountered. This faith in another person finds expression in
statements. We are not in control in this relationship. We have
no other power than the power to accept faith, and we experience it as a gift and grace. "Christ is God encountering us
as "thou," and given to us in person. Faith is the awareness
of this personal encounter, the knowledge and acknowledg-
ment of God who seeks and claims us for himself in Christ."
These words are Brunner's but not (as he supposes) the opposite of the Catholic view; they are wholly in accord with it.

The "other supernatural way" is defined not merely as God's
self-revelation, but as the revealing of "the eternal decrees of
his will." These cannot be derived from creation, nor from
man's reflection upon himself, but are based upon the freedom
of God, and tend in a quite specific way to be realized and
expressed in history. The words "the eternal decrees of his will"
—found in the First Vatican text quoted early in this chapter
—should go towards excluding a one-sided, intellectualist
interpretation of supernatural revelation, that is, an interpretation of revelation as though it were a mere thing. The council
demands an understanding which perceives in supernatural
revelation an activity of God, expressed in particular acts and
events, in history. This means not that the content and the
truths of the revelation which has taken place in history are
disputed or denied, but that they are seen within the whole of
revelation, so that the fact and the substance of revelation are
united. If we look for a more precise account of the eternal
decrees of God's will we find that they consist of the saving
events willed and ordained by God in the old and new covenants, fulfilled by Jesus Christ, yet still awaiting their ultimate
consummation.

However we look at it, the Catholic understanding of revelation in its authentic and complete form can be free from

one-sided intellectualism and can also contain that personal and historical emphasis which it has often been the virtue of Protestant theology to assert.

Our summary of the concept of revelation within the framework of present-day theology would be incomplete if it did not take into account the conception of revelation in what is commonly known as existential theology. The standard expression of this theology is given by Rudolf Bultmann.

In his well-known essay "The Concept of Revelation in the New Testament," Bultmann explains that an idea which prepares the way for revelation is to be found in everyday life in the form of the disclosure of what is concealed, either through the imparting of knowledge, making known to us what was unknown, or by an event which alters our existence. This understanding of revelation is present in those world religions which have a doctrine of revelation. But what it implies in these religions is a disclosing of what is veiled and concealed, but absolutely necessary to man. That the disclosing is exclusively accorded to religion means that man cannot attain to this revelation—and therefore to his own proper being (his "salvation")—himself; it must be given to him. This fact displays an understanding of existence aware of the finite condition of man. In seeking for revelation it discloses this finite condition. Consequently, revelation (and knowledge about it) is intrinsic to the life and existence of man himself. The answer to the question of what revelation is—and the question implies that only a preparatory conception of revelation, but not a true understanding of it exists as yet—can be found only if the inquirer is ready for his own finite condition to be disclosed. In this way Bultmann prepares the way for the understanding of what revelation means theologically, especially in the New Testament.

The New Testament asks what is the finite condition, and it answers that what limits man is death, not merely as the end of life, but as a constant threat to the whole of existence. Man revolts against this existential peril for his own existence, and at the same time experiences his inability to control death. In face of this situation, the limit and finite condition laid down by death which makes life meaningless, the only possible meaning of revelation is that of the destruction of death by life. This, Bultmann concludes, is in fact the message of the New Testament: "Death is swallowed up in victory." Christ is the resurrection and the life.

However, this New Testament message is not already present within the world. On the contrary, for death leads beyond the world. Only faith is aware of this message and the eschatological mode of existence revealed in it. Only faith can tolerate the paradox that the life which is spoken of does not appear as life but as the enhancement of death (2 Corinthians 6, 9 f.). The revelation of life and death which is encountered in what took place in Christ and in the cross is a concealed revelation, made present in the form of the Word, uttered in preaching here and now, and accepted in faith.

The life revealed in the New Testament can be described in other terms, particularly by the concept of "God righteousness." This consists in man's acquittal from sin, which is vouchsafed by God. Sin here means above all man's attempt to understand himself on the basis of his own being, to provide his own assurance, to glorify himself and to forget that man is a creature.

Death as the "wages of sin" is the settlement and the punishment for such an attitude. In sin, man regards death as what is true, ultimate, and "existing for death." In this situation, revelation cannot mean the denial of death, but is regarded as a preliminary; it is not death, but God, who is understood as the limit, and to accept death as the "first step" towards him. The limit and finite condition which is called death is thereby swallowed up in the—eternal—life which God gives.

That God does give this life is the message of the revelation of the New Testament, the word which tells of Christ and of what took place in him. But what takes place therein is the restoration of the origin of all things, creation, together with its revelation. In Jesus, the true and second Adam, life based on God and lived by God was manifested. This life is the possibility which man can apprehend, in freedom as it is properly understood, and which indeed he must apprehend.

Bultmann sums up his theology of revelation in the well-known words: "What is revealed? *Nothing at all*, if revelation is looking for doctrines, doctrines to which no man could have attained, and mysteries, which once they have been imparted, will be known once for all. Yet *everything* is revealed, insofar as man's eyes are opened to himself; once again he can understand himself."[4]

This concept of revelation has an impressive coherence. And revelation, as the revelation of God to man, is both the basis and constantly present factor of human existence. This is expressed in Bultmann's saying: to speak of God (to speak of the revelation of God) is to speak of man; to speak of man is to speak of God.

Both Catholic and Protestant theology ask the following questions of Bultmann's understanding of revelation. Does this exclusively existential understanding of revelation make it possible to describe everything which is the word, history of salvation, to which the Old and New Testaments bear witness? Does not the fullness of the concrete and many-sided content of revelation, in history and in various forms in word, belong essentially and intrinsically to revelation? What of the absolute sovereignty of God's action, which is not exhausted by man's attainment of his own proper being? What of the figure of the person of Jesus Christ, which is not identical either with the "Christ event" or Christian with preaching about it? Bultmann

[4] *Glauben und Verstehen,* III (Tübingen, 1960), p. 27.

39

neglects all this. Does not Bultmann's starting-point link between death and life, existential understanding, beg the question of what revelation is? The ultimate question is: Are revelation and faith necessary in order to give man the existential understanding of himself which Bultmann outlines? Is not what took place in Christ, together with the kerygma, superfluous?

In any case, the previous pages have served to show that a successful dialogue is possible within Catholic and Protestant theology today on revelation.

II. THE TWO FORMS AND WAYS IN WHICH REVELATION IS REALIZED IN THE LIGHT OF SCRIPTURE

Here we are not concerned with a philological and terminological study of the word and concept of revelation as it occurs in the Bible, but to work out from the testimony of the Bible to what the term refers. Many words are used in the Bible to refer to revelation. This reflects the multiplicity of what revelation means, a multiplicity not merely of content, but of historical events. As the Bible understands it, this variety makes it possible to perceive the coherence and plan of the revelation to which it bears witness, the coordination and interrelationship of its various aspects, the οἰκονομία, of salvation.

A. Revelation in Creation

The biblical testimony to "natural" revelation can be described not so much as a carefully balanced treatise, but rather as a drama with acts and interludes. This drama is particularly evident in the classical account of the revelation of God in creation: "For the wrath of God is revealed from heaven against all ungodliness and wickedness of men who by their wickedness suppress the truth. For what can be known about God is plain to them, because God has shown it to them. Ever since the creation of the world his invisible nature, namely, his eternal power and deity, has been clearly perceived in the

41

things that have been made. So they are without excuse; for although they knew God they did not honor him as God or give thanks to him, but they became futile in their thinking and their senseless minds were darkened. Claiming to be wise, they became fools, and exchanged the glory of the immortal God for images resembling mortal man or birds or animals or reptiles" (Romans 1, 18–23). Let us attempt to distinguish the different elements in what this passage tells us.

The agent of the initial revelatory act is God. (Romans 1, 20) says he is an invisible, hidden God. But he has come out of his concealment into unconcealment.

The invisible God has made himself visible through the works of his creation from the creation of the world (ἀπὸ κτίσεως κόσμου through the ποιήματα). God, as the creator, stands in contrast to his work, the cosmos. He is distinguished from what he has made. Creation is not nature (φύσις) derived from itself or existing from eternity, but a work brought into being by God. It has a beginning, and receives its origin and nature from the creator. The world is God's; it is not the dominion of gods. The idea of the creation is contrasted to that of myth, insofar as the latter places on the same level the world and the gods, theogony and cosmogony, the history and destiny of the world and that of the gods. From this point of view, a myth of creation is a contradiction in terms. What exists can be seen to be created. God manifests himself in this created existence; he who is hidden reveals himself, and he who is invisible becomes somewhat visible.

Through this revelation, man too comes to understand himself as a creature, a creature who knows and acknowledges the creator. Man derives his being from a source. By knowing that he and the world are creatures, man knows of God.

God discloses himself and makes himself known. Some knowledge of God is given to man before and outside God's specific and special revelation. This much can be known, and

42

can be seen with the νοῦς τὰ ἀόρατα νοούμενα καθορᾶται. Paul mentions two aspects of this γνωστὸν τοῦ θεοῦ: God eternal power and his deity, δύναμις and θειότης.

These ideas from Romans go back to a text in the Book of Wisdom. This book is the most recent of the Old Testament, composed in the first century B.C. in Egypt (probably in Alexandria) by a Hellenistic Jew. It was written in opposition to the religious practice of Egypt, especially to the cults of animals and stars that were practiced there. It is supposed that in the passage quoted above, Paul consciously alluded to Wisdom. After a long description of the foolishness of the Egyptian worship of idols, Wisdom continues, "For all men who were ignorant of God were foolish by nature; and they were unable from the good things that are seen to know him who exists, nor did they recognize the craftsman while paying heed to his works; but they supposed that either fire or wind or swift air, or the circle of the stars, or turbulent water, or the luminaries of heaven were the gods that rule the world. If through delight in the beauty of these things man assumed them to be gods, let them know how much better than these is their Lord, for the author of beauty created them. And if men were amazed at their power and working, let them perceive from them how much more powerful is he who formed them. For from the greatness and beauty of created things comes a corresponding perception of their Creator" (13, 1–5).

There is a further passage which is of equal importance. This is the revelation of the will of God which makes itself known in man himself. Paul discusses this idea elsewhere in the Epistle to the Romans: "When Gentiles who have not the [Mosaic] law do by nature [φύσει] what the law requires, they are a law to themselves, even though they do not have the [Mosaic] law. They show that what the law requires is written on their hearts, while their conscience also bears witness and their conflicting thoughts accuse or perhaps excuse

43

them on that day when . . . God judges the secrets of men . . ." (2, 14–16).

Here too, we can speak of a revelation of God, the making known of his will in a law written into the hearts of men. It is the revelation of the creator in the creature, the revelation of a holy and righteous will which can be known from the con- science which is present in man. It is legitimate to speak of a revelation here, for this "natural law within man" is presented as parallel to the Mosaic law which was explicitly proclaimed and revealed by God. The law written in the heart cor- responds to that written upon the tables of stone; the content of both is similar. The Gentiles do the works of the Mosaic law, "by nature," that is, on the basis of their human nature so created by God. In both cases, the phenomenon of the law goes back to something which is not derived from man, not laid down by him, but is ordained for him and for his sake by God. Its function is to lay an obligation upon man. Conscience bears witness to it, especially in the "conflicting thoughts" which guide the conscience in its judicial task, and "accuse or perhaps excuse them" (Romans, 2, 15). God is the author of this aspect of man's nature, which expresses itself in conscience as a moral imperative and judgment; it points to God and his commands and requirements.

It must however be emphasized that it is repeatedly stated that the revelation of God in creation and in man is not be- lieved but "known and seen": νοούμενα καθορᾶται. Revelation depends upon what is visible to the human eye. We can see that creation is created and that conscience dictates. The mind of man can know from this and in this revelation the creator and Lord, the power and deity of God, his righteousness and holiness.

We said that the biblical doctrine of revelation could be likened to a drama; its second act is played by man. However, the part that is played by man is his failure to live up to the possibilities bestowed upon him by God. Paul (and in its own way, the Book of Wisdom) clearly emphasizes this contrast, and makes quite evident what man has made, as a matter of historical fact of the revelation of God proffered to him in creation. The failure of man is the dominant theme of the first two chapters of Romans, in which the guilt of men, Jews and Gentiles, is described in dismal terms. Paul means that human reality is in revolt against this possibility given to man by God. The existential nature of man as a paradoxical being, the failure of his being and situation, are in revolt. This process takes place in the following stages.

Men have suppressed the truth by their wickedness and have thereby shown themselves to be godless and unrighteous beings. This assertion is valid if creation is an act of God's self-revelation. The actions of man can then be interpreted as a wilful refusal, a conscious perversion of this revelation; they are not merely described as a regrettable failure. The way in which Romans poses the problem must be carefully noted. It does not say that although men could have known God, they did not know him, but that "although they knew God," they did not acknowledge him, but suppressed the truth. Therein lies the guilt of man, and his rebellious attitude towards creation.

The suppression of the truth by wickedness is shown in the fact that men have not acknowledged the God whom they knew, did not honor him or give thanks to him, but tried to live by their own powers, and to be dependent only on themselves, their own actions and works, their own achievements. Honor and thanksgiving are an essential part of knowing God; if it does not have this effect and consequence, it is not the knowledge of God. Because man refuses obedience, he is guilty, and in Paul's eyes without excuse. Consequently, man loses his own true being and becomes prey to lies and untruths concerning himself.

Now the consequence of this action is that men have "become futile in their thinking and their senseless minds were darkened." They have exchanged the truth for nothingness, for vanity, for the foolishness of their own thoughts. "Claiming to be wise, they became fools." What is alleged to be wisdom is darkness for the mind, vanity and pride. Consequently (this is the Pauline theological reflection to which we have already referred), man's foolishness and *hubris* is able to encounter the divine wisdom only in the form of self-emptying, condescension, and foolishness, the foolishness of the cross (1 Corinthians 1, 18), the *kenosis* of Jesus Christ even to death (Philippians 2, 7).

The other form of this guilty confusion which man has brought into being is the exchanging of God the creator for worthless idols (Romans 1, 23). In this confusion of God for idols lies the great deception of man. The statement of Romans concerning man and what he has made of God's revelation in creation is unequivocal; man has perverted the possibility given to him through the revelation of God in creation. But as a result man has also done wrong against himself and his true nature.

We would not be doing justice, however, to the whole biblical discussion of man with regard to the revelation of God in the work of his creation, if we listened only to these assertions. There are others which give a different judgment of man and of what he has made of the revelation in creation in his religion.

The Book of Wisdom says that in believing in false gods men have erred, but adds that they are not wholly and exclusively blameworthy: "For perhaps they go astray while seeking God and daring to find him. For as they live among his works they keep searching, and they trust in what they see, because the things that are seen are beautiful" (13, 6 f.) An even more positive assessment is found within the New Testament in Paul's sermon on the Areopagus (Acts 17). Admittedly, the first impression which the many images of the Greek religion made upon Paul in Athens was disturbing; "his spirit was provoked!" The dominant emotion present is the same as that of Romans. But in his sermon on the Areopagus Paul seeks for something positive in what is negative, a remnant of truth in the chaos of error, the true God among the idols. At the very beginning of his speech he sensed this positive element of doubt: "You are δεισιδαιμονέστεροι." This is not, as Barth says in his comment on this passage, a reproach, but an acknowledgement: "You are very religious." The second positive point Paul sees in the inscription on the altar: "to an unknown God" or "to the unknown God." Paul alludes to the inscription and interprets it in a bold and original way. The Athenians are unconsciously worshipping the true God, who is still unknown to them. The Apostle proclaims the Gospel of the true God, culminating in the event that took place in Christ. But he does not, as in Romans, demonstrate the guilt of pagan religion and polytheism, or describe the moral and social deterioration and perversion of human nature which results from it. Instead, Paul seeks to isolate authentic traces of the unknown God which are to be found in Hellenistic religion and polytheism, and to develop the Gospel of the true and living God leading up to the proclamation of salvation in Jesus Christ. God has shown himself to be the creator of men, the guide of the historical destiny of nations, and the giver of the fruitfulness of the earth (as was described in the sermon in Lystra [Acts 14]: "What therefore you worship as unknown, this I proclaim to you"). The whole speech is a classical example of the link between correlation and the kerygma, between correlation and contradiction.

These words express another important point of view by their description of man and their characterization of the human religion that is based upon the natural revelation in

47

creation. Both points of view must be accepted as the explicit and valid testimony of the New Testament. This is true, whether or not the sermon on the Areopagus is authentic, whether or not it is in fact Paul's.

The third act in the drama of the revelation of God in his creation and the attitude of man towards it is once again determined by God from the account of the Epistle to the Romans. God responds, as a wrathful God. The wrath of God consists in God's "giving man up," abandoning him in his revolt, his self-sought godlessness, his unrighteousness, his perversion and idolatry. God leaves man to his rebellion, he "abandons him to what is at work within him."[5]

But this condition is in no way "natural" to man; it is a perverted state. This perversion consists primarily in the exchanging of creator for creature, of God for idols. As a consequence, man perverts the order of his own nature, and declines into what is unnatural from the bodily, sexual, legal, and social point of view (Romans 1, 26–30). The ultimate perversion is that man approves and applauds those who practice such things (Romans 1, 32).

This description of the actual situation of man and of what he has made of the possibility of the revelation by God in his works does not include everything that Paul has to say. There is a turning point: "All have sinned and fall short of the glory of God" (Romans 3, 23). "But now the righteousness of God has been manifested apart from law" (3, 21), and this is the righteousness which comes through faith in Jesus Christ, righteousness for all who believe.

The words "but now" refer to the eschatological moment in the final revelation of salvation, brought about by Jesus Christ for all men, Jews and Gentiles. In the light of what has happened "now," salvation in Christ, Paul looks back in the first two chapters of Romans to the world before and without

[5] O. Kuss, *Der Römerbrief* (Regensburg, 1957), pp. 42 f.

Christ. A gloomy picture is drawn by one standing in the light. The more brightly the light of ultimate salvation shines for him, the darker the conditions of evil, without salvation, appear. The more the period before Christ appears dark and without grace, the more brightly shines the glory of God revealed in Christ. In this final act brought about by God, the revelation of his righteousness in Jesus Christ, the possibilities for man and creation are realized anew in the divine revelation. The revelation of God in creation is seen with new eyes; the book of creation is read as a book of God. The revelation and offer of God in creation are realized in a new way in Jesus Christ and through faith in him (2 Corinthians 4, 6). The glory of God the creator (and of the dawn of creation) is reflected in the face of Jesus Christ.

The biblical testimony to the revelation of God in creation, and to the creation as the revelation of God, is complex. God has borne testimony to himself in creation, in the cosmos, and above all in man himself. Men have scarcely responded to this possibility at all; they have failed, fallen into error and sin, drawn guilt upon themselves. This error and failure has numerous forms and stages. Yet the Bible bears witness that the error conceals a genuine desire to seek and find, a longing expressed in the idea of the unknown and distant God. The error, the perversion, and the idolatry are second. What comes first is the true nature of man, the truth, the light, the possibility of a man's realization—for us the saving encounter with the God who reveals himself in creation. This is a standard against which perversion and error are judged.

From the actual concrete historical situation there arises in each case the call: Repent! "Turn away from the night of godlessness and unrighteousness, which is without grace, turn away from dumb and empty idols and turn to the 'living and true god'" (1 Thessalonians 1, 9). *Metanois* also includes an additional assertion: "What you worship as unknown, this

I proclaim to you." *Metanoia* can signify the way from an unconscious longing to clear knowledge, from the unknown God to the true God, from the glimmerings of the light to him who says, "I am the light" (John 8, 12).

The salvation manifested and given to us in Christ by grace, the righteousness of God, is a judgment upon everything that preceded and is outside Christ. But it is also the redemption, the gathering in and the fulfilment of everything in the world which, before and outside Christ, is manifested as hope, questioning, and longing. This answers how it is possible to speak of revelation in human religion and in the concrete world-religions outside the supernatural, Christian, and historical revelation. The positive relationship to religion can be seen from our discussion of revelation in creation.

B. Revelation in the Special History of Salvation

The revelation of which the Scriptures speaks and to which it bears witness is not exhausted in natural revelation, in God's revelation, in the creation, and in man. Natural revelation defines the sphere into which a special, historical revelation comes, it describes the connecting link and starting point which is the prerequisite and condition of this new, special revelation.

In Romans the words "but now" referring to revelation and salvation in Jesus Christ mark a break not only from the situation of the Gentiles, but also from that of the Jews. The reason why the Jews are explicitly mentioned is that by comparison with the Gentiles they have something unique— a special message and decree of God, a special calling and election culminating historically in Jesus Christ; they also mark the event of Jesus Christ in history.

If we ask where this special revelation given to the Jews

begins, Scripture gives an unequivocal answer: with the revelation of God to Abraham. It is possible to give an approximate location in time and space: Mesopotamia at the beginning of the second millennium before Christ. This is the historical and geographical setting of the event described in the twelfth chapter of Genesis, the calling and the command of God to Abraham, where the account of the history extending up to Jesus Christ (known by the term "the Old Testament") begins.

Still, the Old Testament does not begin with the calling of Abraham; that is preceded by the all-inclusive conception of the pre-Israelite universal history of the world and mankind. This is the subject of the first eleven chapters of Genesis. The history of creation and mankind's origins given there does not merely provide the setting within which the special revelation to Abraham took place, but also shows what made the calling of Abraham and the revelation given to him meaningful, even necessary.

1. REVELATION AS ORIGIN

The history of the origins of the world and man which forms the beginning of the Scriptures was composed relatively late —probably during the period of the Kings, and in reaction against contemporary myths and mythologies, especially those of Babylon. As the Dutch theologian Henry Renckens has convincingly shown, and as is generally agreed, this history is "Israel's vision of the past." The first eleven chapters of Genesis form a literary, prophetic, and cultic document, drawn from various traditions, which tells what Israel thought about the beginning of the world and of man what it thought on the basis of its concrete, historical, and specific experience with God. It is an account born of living experience, the theological reflection, and divine illumination. Genesis 1–11 is "etiology," an account of origins and causes on the basis of the understanding of what now exists, a prophecy about the past. At the same time, importantly, it provides the outline of a theological anthropology. It contains a description of what man is from his origins. Genesis says that since creation, and through it, there is a revelation of God to man which man can perceive and understand.

But this is not the entire message of the history of origins. The book of Genesis especially in the so-called second creation story (2, 4b–25) and in the story of Paradise (3) tells that man is constituted in a way which goes beyond his reality as a creature. Man has been given a special and gracious self-manifestation of God, and is allowed to share the intimate presence, friendship, and love of God. This situation described in the image of the garden of Paradise forms part of the revelation at the beginning of human history. It, too, must be understood in an etiological sense as Israel's view of its past and that of man.

The departure for this view is an historical and concrete experience: that of human guilt, suffering, evil, sorrow, and death, and their theology, as well as the problem of meaning in history and the constitution of man (who paradoxically is the noblest work of creation and at the same time is in revolt against creation and has defected from it). The image of Paradise describes the opposite of this situation, a different world without shadows and suffering, a world of peace and the close presence of God. This is the world which was destined for man. The present world and situation of mankind can be regarded as a loss of Paradise. This loss took place through an act of man, by his decision against his created and dependent being—in biblical terms by rebellion, the refusal of obedience, and unbelief, by his arrogant attempt to "be like God," to put himself in God's place, "knowing good and evil"

(Genesis 3, 5). Paradise lost means that man falls back through his own guilt into a created condition which is broken and damaged and which provides the historical and concrete situation in which he finds himself at any given time: he is man in revolt, who has lost his own true being and is fallen. The first sin, however, has not merely blighted the past but marks the present time; it represents the decision taken by man against God which is always with him and is constantly renewed. Sin today is seen in the light of the past.

Chapters 4–11 of Genesis paint a drastic picture of the increasingly deteriorating situation brought about by the "increase of sin." Of course, there are figures in the story which relieve the general gloom: Abel, Enoch, and Noah.

The covenant with Noah (Genesis 6) is an affirmation and renewal of the possibility which man still possesses of knowing God from creation. Man can understand creation, the life and fruitfulness found in the rhythm of the year and the seasons, as a gift made to him, recognizing it as a revelation and manifestation of the divine, and acknowledging this recognition in the form of religion. The Acts of the Apostles refers to this situation when it says, ". . . God who made the heaven and the earth and the sea and all that is in them . . .) did not leave himself without witness, for he did good and gave you from heaven rains and fruitful seasons, satisfying your hearts with food and gladness" (14, 15–17.)

The world-religions are the historical expression and concrete form taken by the "religion" originally present in every man; they are based—from the theological point of view—on the assumptions and conditions described above yet expressed in various ways. Consequently, the religions of humanity possess the character of revelation. At the same time, they provide visible and richly varied evidence of what men have made of religion in the course and throughout the development of history, positively and negatively. Through particularly intensive apprehensions and experiences of these complex modes of God's revelation, some men have been able to found religions and religious societies. Nature and cosmic religions are positive and negative answers to a revelation through creation. The religions of law are a sign and testimony of the revelation of God in conscience. Religions of redemption are induced by the phenomenon of creation, Paradise (the Golden Age), guilt and punishment (the loss of Paradise), together with the longing for redemption, deliverance and salvation. This perspective gives us a final and ultimate understanding of the religions of mankind.

The historical and religious situation of man is the necessary preliminary to the special historical revelation of God which began with the calling of Abraham.

2. REVELATION AS PROMISE

a. Revelation in the History of the Old Testament Covenant

God's special historical revelation begins with Abraham. The first cosmic and then historical setting quickly grows narrower; the beginnings of mankind's universal history is replaced by the particular and distinctive calling of one nation.

The beginning of this special historical revelation, the patriarchal history, also has an etiological purpose. This is to see a pattern and basis in the exemplary figures of the patriarchs for the origin and early stages of the history of Israel: guidance, care for and election by God, the call to be different from other nations, faith as the basis of the nation's existence.

The revelation beginning with Abraham is appropriately known as "revelation in the form of promise."[6] This definition shows what is new in this form of revelation. What corre-

---

[6] Brunner, *op. cit.,* p. 98.

sponds to the promise on man's side is not knowledge, but faith and obedience. A promise is rooted in history. This explains the title which is given to the figure of Abraham throughout the whole Scripture, that of the father of faith, and explains why all true believers, Jews and Gentiles, are known as the children of Abraham. Faith, not physical descent, constitutes and marks the true children of Abraham (see Galatians 3, 6 ff.; Romans 4, 1 ff.; John 8, 33).

The history of Abraham shows what God's special revelation, Judaeo-Christian salvation history, is. His life and destiny followed the word, will, and act of a God who comes to the individual, and in so doing discloses himself and the eternal decrees of his saving will. The history of Abraham provides the model for the other patriarchal histories, and the basic structure of God's acts, God's guidance, and man's answer.

The patriarchal histories describe the special way in which the people of Israel came into existence and began its historical course, as a people given to God for his own. Consequently, the patriarchal histories are not simply historical accounts, but kerygma, a prophecy about the past, but also a doxology of history uttered with the present time in mind. The present time is seen as the fruit of the promise, understood on the basis of God's act of revelation, and through faith.

The history of the founding of the people of Israel contains the same features which were present in outline in patriarchal history, and especially in the life of Abraham. It has the same characteristics and follows the same laws, but on a larger scale. The second decisive action of historical revelation takes place with the calling of Moses in Egypt, a highly civilized country both in politics and religion. The time is that of Pharaoh Rameses II (1298–1225 B.C.). His outstanding predecessor, Amenophis IV, was the founder of the religion of the sun god worshipped as the sole lord and creator of all things. But after the death of this king, and at the time of Moses, the old polytheist and theriomorphic religion underwent a revival. The calling of Moses takes place in the theophany described in Exodus (2, 1 ff.). It culminates in the revelation of the name of God (2, 74). The purpose of this revelation is not to obtain a magical control over God; God is to be called upon by his name. The revelation of the name of God, which is identified with the God of the Fathers (*Ēl, Ēl Šaddai;* see Exodus 6, 2) is: "I am who I am" — "I am present," "This is my name for ever, and thus I am to be remembered throughout all generations" (Exodus 3, 14 f.). This "I am," an interpretation of the new and distinctive divine name Yahweh, is a message. It signifies that "No holy place, no mountain, and no temple is the resting place of the God who sent Moses. He is not stationary; he is present, he is present here and now in the history of Israel. 'I am present' does not mean merely 'I exist' (the existence of God); nor merely 'I am everywhere in space' (the omnipresence of God). God is not speaking of his nature when he reveals himself to Moses as 'I am,' but of his active, interested presence: Pharaoh will see, even though he will not acknowledge, that there is now someone mightier than he ruling in his land. Israel, enslaved and condemned to be exterminated, will experience this awareness, and see its liberator and redeemer at work. The invisible is 'visibly' manifested in historical acts, he is revealed in the ordinary and universal course of human history."[7]

The promise given to Moses was fulfilled in the liberation of the people from the slavery of Egypt and in the series of miraculous acts associated with it. The Bible testifies that these events in the history of the people of Israel, the historical occurrences which constituted the nation and brought it into being, are in no way purely the result of the natural, political interaction of events, but with their accumulation of paradox,

[7] F. Stier, *Geschichte Gottes mit den Menschen* (Düsseldorf, 1962), p. 22.

contradicting all human expectation, calculation, and imagining, are the consequence of God's guidance, providence, election, power, and glory. The revelation of God has been realized in effective action in this history. Consequently, this history can be understood and interpreted as the revelation of God, as the place in which the assurances and promises of God are fulfilled. For this reason, these events were henceforth constantly "remembered" and celebrated in the cult. Here Israel made an explicit and appropriate confession of faith in what had taken place, glorifying it in the assertion that Yahweh had led Israel out of Egypt in a miraculous way. This single historical act became the underlying foundation of the faith of Israel, and the constantly renewed assurance of Yahweh's saving assistance and redeeming power in the present and in the future. An event which had taken place on one occasion became the guarantee and promise of what was to come, an ever new basis for faith and hope.

The people of Israel, founded and guided in such a unique way, now became the partner in a new, greater covenant, which the God who saved the people out of Egypt made with them. This gave form to the election of his people, as well as to the revelation laid upon them. "You have seen what I did to the Egyptians, and how I bore you on eagles' wings and brought you to myself. Now therefore, if you will obey my voice and keep my covenant, you shall be my own possession among all peoples; for all the earth is mine, and you shall be to me a kingdom of priests and a holy nation" (Exodus 19, 4–6).

These words are the proclamation of Yahweh as king in Israel: God is choosing Israel to be his peculiar people, to be a kingdom of priests. This is the first occurrence of the term "kingdom," of the kingly rule of God.

The solemn agreement of the covenant, the foundation of the kingly rule of God, is described in Scripture in most dramatic terms (later solemnly celebrated in the memorial of the events of Sinai at the feast of the Passover [Exodus 23, 14 ff.]): the theophany on the mountain, the proclamation of the royal law through Moses, the people's oath of obedience.

The Decalogue, the ten commandments, which are God's royal law given on Sinai, lays down the basic relationship of the people of Israel to God; the *tōrāh* beginning with the affirmation of monotheism (Exodus 20, 2–3) is the great and special revelation of God to his own people. It distinguishes this people from other nations and religions. Israel must preserve its separation and distinctiveness; it must not become like other nations: "You shall not do as they do in the land of Egypt, where you dwelt, and you shall not do as they do in the land of Canaan, to which I am bringing you" (Leviticus 18, 3). The conclusion and consummation of the acts of revelation and liberation towards the people of Israel, is the entry into Canaan, the details of which are not easy to elucidate. An important element here is the covenant at Shechem, which is concluded with Joshua, the successor of Moses.

The existential question which concerned the people of Israel in Canaan was whether Israel was to remain faithful to its calling and commission not to be like the other nations, but to trust in God alone, and have him alone as Lord, or whether it had failed him and refused to serve him. The biblical account tells how in Canaan the nation succumbed to the temptation to be like other nations—even from the *religious* point of view. Its calling and election was largely forgotten: in Canaan, Israel often became like the "nations of the world," or in biblical language it "turned" from Yahweh, "left" its God, and "forgot the covenant of Yahweh."

The struggle between assimilation and separation, and the conflict between God and the idols, between Yahweh and Baal, reached its climax in the demand of Elijah to the priests and prophets of Baal: "If the Lord is God, follow him; but if Baal, then follow him" (1 Kings 18, 21). The second assimilation of the chosen people to their environment took place in the political sphere. The kingly rule of Yahweh over his people was first exercised directly. God, the spirit of God, stirred up men who came to the assistance of the nation in its hour of need. The judges became the nation's leaders. This free form of rule laid great emphasis on the sovereignty of God as the king of Israel. The power and strength of this king became the power and strength of his people. It was a charismatic theocracy, giving theocratic charisma. But it did not last. The separation of the people of God was not maintained, for it offered no possibilities for practical power politics. The call grew stronger for a permanent institutional government and a visible representation of the people. The efforts made to obtain this government ultimately forced Samuel, the last of the judges, to make the decision that "we will have a king over us, that we also may be like all the nations, and that our king may govern us and go out before us and fight our battles" (1 Samuel 8, 19 f.). As in their religion, the people of Israel also sought to "be like all the nations" in their politics. What from a purely empirical and political point of view had the appearance of a natural and normal development, in which a federation of tribes became an organized state, was from the point of view of faith a decline of the nation from the rule of God.

However, this new departure, the adoption under duress of the monarchy, was taken over and articulated into the law of the people of God—this was the beginning of a new experiment—and it was done in such a way that the basic principle of the covenant and the promise was maintained. "You shall be my people, and I will be your God." This command could be realized even within the monarchy; the intention was that the monarchy should be the organ and instrument of the kingdom of God. What was begun here seemed to have succeeded

59

in the person and the kingdom of David. He brought the tribes of Israel together, and through successful military campaigns created a powerful empire. The unity of the people was based upon Yahweh, who was the common God of them all. David expressed the links that bound them together by transferring the Ark of the Covenant, with the tables of the law, the document of the covenant with God, to Jerusalem, to Mount Zion. There, next to the royal palace, the temple was to be set up in place of the tabernacle that had preceded it: the one God was to be king over the nation's king.

The climax of the life of David meant at the same time a turning point in the history of the monarchy in Israel. Two lines of assimilation crossed at this point: a horizontal line, that of assimilation to the surrounding world, and a vertical line, along which the new historical development, the building of the temple and the dynasty—ominous innovations which followed from the natural course of events—were dovetailed into God's plans. Both contained hidden dangers. The building of the temple brought the danger of changing the God who "accompanies the people on their journeys" (Martin Buber), who "is present, wherever he wishes to be present," into a stationary deity, dwelling in a temple like other gods, no longer present under no one's control but his own, but instead constantly accessible at a given place. The other innovation, hereditary succession to the throne, also led to the dangerous path of assimilation. In the case of Saul and David, the "Spirit of Yahweh" played an important part in their being chosen as king. But now the charisma, the authority which no one could take upon himself, which was only accorded to a chosen person, and which inspired him to show valor in war and to rule, was replaced by the "house," the dynasty.

In the context of our present theme we cannot discuss the historical course and development of this new stage and form of revelation which the monarchy presents. Seen as a whole, it was not successful. Israel's flirtation with worldly power, and the attempt to preserve and manifest in the world its distinctive characteristic, its election, failed.

But we must take into account another phenomenon of this period of the monarchy (900–500 B.C.), that of prophecy. The prophets of Israel form a counterbalance to the monarchy and to the priesthood with its dangers and constant temptations. Yet the priesthood had its temptations, being satisfied with external rituals, neglecting faith and morals in the process. The prophets are as distinct from the prophetic figures of other religions as Yahweh is from their gods. They are explicitly linked with certain kings: Elijah with Ahab, Isaiah with Ahaz, Jeremiah with Jehoiakim and Zedekiah, as well as being opposed to the representatives of the official priesthood of the time. What is a prophet? A prophet is one who (from the original meaning of the word) speaks in place of another; he acts under orders. A prophet is one who is "stirred up," separated, called and chosen by God. A prophet is one who sees, another word used to describe the prophet, a "seer." The vision of the prophet does not reach in the first instance into the past and the future, but into the immediate present. The prophet sees, recognizes, and tells how the affairs of God are being dealt with by the people, the king, and the priests. The eye of a prophet is not blinded by the fact that everything is apparently in order and that all tasks are being carried out. He sees the empty lack of faith and love behind the outward façade, and recognizes evil in the midst of the outward salvation proclaimed by the court prophets, the false prophets. On the other hand, he comforts the people in the face of misfortune, exile, and hopelessness. A prophet is one who tells with courage and authority what is at issue in a given historical situation. The prophet stands up for his word and his mission and is ready to seal his word through his life and his deeds. The task of the prophet consists in guarding and inculcating the

61

truth of the covenant in the face of every attempt to replace the covenant of God by a political covenant.

The prophet Jeremiah determines salvation history during the greatest catastrophe of Israel's history, the siege and destruction of Jerusalem; Ezekiel's word determines the captivity in Babylon itself. With this disaster, one period in the history of God's dealings with men comes to an end—a period which, it must be repeatedly emphasized, was not characterized by political or historical process but by a dialogue between God and his people. This dialogue failed not because it was bound to, but because it was rejected by man. History does not only take place, it is carried out in the encounter of God with man, and in the encounter of man with God and with his fellow man. History begins merely to happen only when man lets himself become its prisoner and ceases to live it.

During the period of distress, exile, and foreign rule, the people of God began a process of reflection on these events. What happened? What is going to happen? What are we to do? After the judgement of God upon Israel had been carried out, it would also (according to the prophecy of the time) fall upon other nations. But then the time of salvation would come, a time of liberation and of new life in the kingdom of God. This is the message of the prophets of this period. At the same time, salvation would also begin for all nations: the nations would come and do pilgrimage to the mountain of God (Jeremiah 16, 19; Isaiah 56, 7; Zechariah 2, 14). God, the king of Israel, would be king over all nations. It would be a time in which the blessedness of the earliest days and of Paradise would return (Isaiah 35, 1–10). All flesh would look on the salvation of God, and the coming of God would be the epiphany of the divine king.

But after the return from exile, the nation had once again to face the question, "What have we to do, that the kingdom may come?" This question was reinforced by the experiences undergone in captivity and by what had been maintained during the exile, the remembrance of the history of salvation, and the words of the prophets. The great leaders and reformers, Ezra and Nehemiah, guided the people towards the exact fulfillment of the law which the nation had known since the days of Moses and which had been extended and developed in the course of the centuries. Moreover, a class of teachers of the law was formed from among the people.

The Books of the Maccabees tell of the open religious war which broke out when King Antiochus IV (174–164) forbade the temple sacrifices, the sabbath, and circumcision, ordered the holy scriptures to be destroyed, and forced the Jews under threat of capital punishment to sacrifice to Greek gods. They also tell how while many defected, a small remnant maintained itself in being, the community of a new covenant. It is possible that this is the community which assembled about the Teacher of Righteousness, about which we have learned more from the discoveries at Qumran. This community was preparing itself for the day of God and the coming of his kingdom. "What must we do for the kingdom to come?" The answer of Qumran is compliance with the law in all its severity, and a special rule for their order. With the subjection of the people of Israel to Roman rule their external history as leading to Christ comes to an end.

b. Definition of the Categories
into which the Old Testament Revelation Falls

God communicates himself in the revelation of the Old covenant within various categories.

The basic category in which revelation takes place can be expressed by the Hebrew "dābār." It includes two categories in one: it means the *word* which becomes action, and it means the deed and *action* which precedes from the word. The fundamental data of revelation in the Old Testament are the word and action in a mutual and unified relationship.

God spoke in the acts and events of the history of Israel. The events which took place can and ought to be understood and interpreted in this sense. To do this is the special task and function of the human prophetic word. It would be a misunderstanding, however, to suppose that the events received their significance as revelation and as the Word of God only through the message of the prophets. The events possess this intrinsic significance in themselves, that is, it is inherent in the fact that they are brought about by God. In the message of the prophets their authentic interpretation is brought to light and given explicit utterance. "The prophetic word is based upon the revelation in actions, and the revelation in actions is consummated in the word." But in the same way, it must be said that the Word of God, which is given to man in order to command, instruct, and guide him, is historical in nature, creates history, and becomes effective in history. The task and the activity of the prophets themselves, with Moses at their head, is an impressive example of this role.

Another basic category of Old Testament revelation, besides that of word and action, is the *name* of God; revelation is the revelation of the name of God. The proclamation of the name of God (there are numerous designations for the name of God) means that God has been set up as Lord, protector, and owner of Israel. The name both manifests and conceals the presence and meaning of his person, including the actual person who imparts himself. The name can stand for a person. When the "name of the Lord" is "called upon," this does not mean as in many religions the possession of an ability to control and conjure up the deity, but honors him and his absolute sovereignty.

We must finally refer to another category, which occurs

64

within revelation, and is included in it: that of the *face of God*. "The face of God is God graciously disclosing himself to men, God giving men a part in his divine radiance." The concept of the "face of God" adds something new to the categories of word, action, and name; it refers to the opening or barring of access to God, to the withdrawal of his gracious and glorious presence. This decisive category of the face of God shows with particular clarity that the characteristic of the revelation to which the Old Testament bears testimony is that it is a revelation in the form of a promise. For if we ask when and how the showing and the hiding of the face of God take place, we are perplexed. It is as though the Old Testament sought to point towards something, something not yet for us in full reality, as if it tried to show that it is more promise than event, or, more precisely, that it is an event in the form of a promise. For he of whom we can say, "We have beheld his glory," in whom we see the face of God, and in whom the gracious Word of God directed to us has shone out, is not yet there, but is promised.

c. Definition of the Subjects
of the Old Testament Revelation

We have been calling the form and stage of revelation "revelation in the form of a promise." God reveals himself first as Yahweh, as the God of Israel. He is the one and only Lord, the living God; this he is in an exclusive and incomparable sense (Exodus 20, 3–6). This fundamental idea runs through the whole history of Israel: "Hear, O Israel, the Lord our God is one Lord" (Deuteronomy 6, 4) is the confession of faith uttered every day. The God of Israel reveals himself as the Lord of the history of this people. The history begins with the liberation from Egypt, an event constantly remembered

65

and liturgically celebrated. God's revelation as salvation in history is a mysterious web woven by God's deeds and words, man's response. The revelation that God is Lord is the revelation of God's *glory*, and every way in which God reveals himself is a revelation that he is Lord. Yahweh reveals himself in history as the holy one. God's will is good, and goodness is the demand of Yahweh. This is a basic element of his royal law. "I am the Lord your God . . . be holy, for I am holy" (Leviticus 11, 44). That is why his demand is for justice and righteousness, for obedience, mercy, and love. Yahweh reveals himself as the creator, maintainer, and ruler of the whole world. Slowly, Israel sees that its God is the one God who since the creation has been revealed to the world and to man.

The unique revelation given to Israel resulted in the separation of this people from their environment. This situation was constantly in conflict with a negative tendency undermining, to assimilate to their neighbors, to be "like other nations." But Israel maintained the revelation. What had taken place and was now taking place in Israel was a "sign for the nations." The aim of Israel's exclusiveness is *universality*. Israel has a mediatorial and representative function in behalf of all nations.

Just as the appeal to the past, to past history, was an evident element in the revelation of Israel, so the prophets interpreted the present as the act and decree of God. An even more characteristic feature was the urge towards the future. What was to come was more important than the past and the present; it was revelation in the form of a promise. Every event, however impressive it may be, and however large it might loom in the memory of the nation, pointed beyond itself towards something greater. Even the greatest fulfillment within Israel was still a promise of something to come in the future.

This is true of the figures of revelation: Moses, the judges, the kings, and the prophets. Their message was the same: after us comes one who is greater than we. All the promises in the

Old Testament clearly point beyond the immediate reality. The kingdom in which God's will rules was still to come. The king after God's own heart was still awaited.

In the expectation of him who was to come the expectation and promise of the old covenant was concentrated and took on a concrete form. Numerous elements and themes coincide in this figure and in the form taken at particular times by the expectation of his coming. There is a political aspect. He who is to come will be a king on the pattern of David, but will surpass him in power and in the extent of his rule, and will be king over all nations. Then there are the themes of salvation (Isaiah 7; 9; 11): the Messiah is the Prince of Peace who brings righteousness, mercy, and love. Ezekiel adds the theme of the good shepherd who brings back the strayed sheep, binds up the crippled sheep, and strengthens the weak (Ezekiel 34, especially, 34, 23–31). For Deutero-Isaiah he who is to come is not a king, but the suffering servant of God, who atones for the guilt of the world (Isaiah 42). He appears in a new form in the visions of the Book of Daniel: the great kingdoms of the world are replaced by the kingdom of God, which rules for ever; this kingdom of God is inaugurated by one who has the appearance of a son of man, but who comes from heaven (Daniel 7). The messianic hope (the conjunction of political, religious, and soteriological themes found in it) is typical of the extent to which the revelation through the old covenant is a revelation of promise.

Another element in what we have just described, and a confirmation of it, is the way in which the ordering of time within this form of revelation is regarded. As a general principle it can be said that the framework of revelation is not so much spatial as temporal in nature. The division is not between this world and the world beyond, but between past, present, and future. This understanding of time is particularly true of the revelation in the old covenant. An event takes place here

67

and now. But what is happening now is at the same time the promise of an event to come: what is present always includes something in the future, which is greater, more comprehensive, and more real than what is now. In this way, while every moment in the history of salvation and every event possesses significance in itself, at the same time this significance is relative to what is to come. The picture of time implied by this form and stage of revelation, revelation in the form of a promise, is not that of a circle—the symbol of a closed system which is always the same and constantly recurring, the symbol of myth—but that of a line or a stream of time. In this picture, history is understood as what is new and imminent. But the picture is also meant to express the fact that the past is included in what is new in the form of tradition and continuity.

Does this line run smoothly or is it broken? It runs smoothly insofar as God's Word and act are effected in time and in history, and the "eternal decrees of his will" are realized. But the line runs irregularly, rising and falling, if we look at the outward course of history: success and failure, exaltation and degradation, defection and punishment, repentence and fresh defection. The line of time follows a rising course insofar as the revelation of the old covenant promises something greater, is still to come. In the very decline that takes place in the outward history of Israel, what is to come becomes more and more urgent and clear. The word of prophecy and historical events increasingly towards what is called the fullness of time.

3. REVELATION AS FULFILLMENT

With the Old Testament characterized by the concept of "promise," we necessarily expect the fulfillment of that promise. This fulfillment is the history, event, message, and person to which the writings of the New Testament witness. The significance of the concept of "fulfillment" for the reality and the understanding of revelation may be sought first of all by studying the biblical concept of time.

a. The Fulfillment of Revelation: "Today"

For the old covenant the decisive category is the future: he who is to come. But the New Testament sees the decisive category of time in the present, today, now, the present moment. This "now" has arrived in Jesus Christ. The rising line of time perceivable in the Old Testament has now attained its goal. Time has reached its high point as its end. Mark describes the situation in the well-known words: "The time is fulfilled ($\pi\epsilon\pi\lambda\acute{\eta}\rho\omega\tau\alpha\iota\ \acute{o}\ \kappa\alpha\iota\rho\acute{o}s$), and the kingdom of God is at hand" (1, 15). Paul uses similar language: "But when the time had fully come ($\tau\grave{o}\ \pi\lambda\acute{\eta}\rho\omega\mu\alpha\ \tau o\hat{v}\ \chi\rho\acute{o}\nu o\nu$), God sent forth his Son" (Galatians 4, 4). From another aspect, time has come to its middle point. This middle point can in its turn serve as the origin of what is to follow. But what is to follow can no longer surpass what has preceded it, its decisive middle point.

It is true that for the New Testament understanding of revelation the goal of time is still to come at the end of the ages. In the New Testament the future is a theme which is extensively discussed. Associated with it is a living hope, the coming of the kingdom of God and the coming of the Lord "in power and glory" at the parousia. To this extent there is still a promise. This has a different form, and refers to something different, from the promise which is characteristic of the Old Testament. The ancient liturgical petition "Maranatha" (1 Corinthians 16, 22; Revelations 22, 20) gives permanent expression to this expectation and prayer of the New Testament. But this middle point, or end of time, has come in Jesus Christ. Oscar Cullmann illustrates this fact by a striking (if not particularly attractive) image: "The decisive battle in a war may already have occurred in a relatively early stage of the war, and yet the war still continues. Although the decisive effect of that battle is perhaps not recognized by all, it nevertheless already means victory. But the war must still be carried on for an undefined time, until 'victory day.' Precisely this is the situation of which the New Testament is conscious, as a result of the recognition of the new division of time; the revelation consists precisely in the fact of the proclamation that that event on the cross, together with the resurrection which followed, was the already concluded decisive battle." It is not a contradiction to say that in Jesus Christ the fulfillment has taken place, while at the same time an ultimate end is still awaited. The event of Christ includes both present fulfillment and future expectation, what already is, and what is not yet. If we ask where the decisive point comes, the answer is that it lies in Christ. Only in Christ is it possible to speak of the end and the goal of time. *The present is the future, which has already begun, and the future is the present, brought to its goal.* No other event either before or since Christ possesses the same central significance as that which took place in him.

This corrects the extreme eschatological view advanced by Albert Schweitzer and Martin Werner, who suggested that the whole New Testament possesses only a single tendency or line, a single central point, the parousia of the Lord, so that it is exclusively orientated towards the future. No doubt, the hope of the return of the Lord and the coming of the kingdom of God in power is a living hope within the New Testament. The fact that the primitive Christian hope is even more intense than that of Judaism might be taken to imply that the New Testament placed the eschatology of the future at the center of the event which it describes. But intensity of hope and center are not the same thing, and ought not to be confused. Actually, this intense hope of the parousia can be explained by the fact that a particular historical event has already come about, the coming of Jesus Christ, and that the future has already begun in this event. This means that the hope of the future is based upon faith in the present. What has happened offers a firm guarantee for what will happen. The hope of Jesus Christ's return is based upon the fact that he has already come, and our faith in him. Faith in the fulfillment which has taken place in Christ is the basis for the expectation of the parousia and the hope that it will soon come about. The parousia does not cast its light upon the historical present to which the New Testament bears testimony, but the latter lights the way which leads towards the future. The fulfillment of revelation "today" finds another powerful expression in the New Testament. What has happened once in Christ has happened once for all (Romans 6, 10).

We must avoid a second misunderstanding of this fulfillment which took place in the revelation of the new covenant. This misunderstanding consists in supposing that the Old Testament (in its form of promise it is unquestionably a testimony to Christ) can be identified in detail with the books of the New Testament, so that the Old Testament is not a revelation concerning the period before Christ, but a hidden, mysterious representation of the events, person, and history of Jesus himself. According to this conception, the New Testament is already fundamentally contained in the Old, and is no more than a new version of something already known. The Old Testament and the New Testament became interchangeable. This view is possible only by overlooking the importance of history. The Old Testament represents a different stage, and therefore a different part of the history of salvation. Its full meaning is recognized in relation to its fulfillment in Christ.

71

But this relationship is strictly temporal: the categories of promise and fulfillment are not interchangeable and never identical. Salvation occurs in linear history.

Barth illustrates the relationship between the old and the new covenants by the image, at first illuminating, of the prophet who looks forward and the apostle who looks back: both look towards the same Christ, but the prophet looks forward to him, while the apostle looks back to him. But as Brunner rightly objects, the use of this scheme has a negative effect: time is replaced by space. Forwards and backwards in space is something quite different from before and after in time. Between the prophetic foretelling of Christ and the message of the New Testament there is the difference between what is merely proclaimed in advance, and what has been actually fulfilled. The fulfillment is the same as what is prophesied, in the sense that it is the object of the promise (Jesus can say in the Gospel of John: "Abraham rejoiced that he was to see my day; he saw it and was glad" [John 8, 56]). But at the same time the fulfillment is something quite different. Now it is a present reality, not merely a future which is contemplated. To fail to see this point is to ignore the stages and acts in the drama of the history of salvation, the process of the economy of salvation.

The New Testament regards the present moment, now, today, this hour, "my hour," as of great importance; the distinctive mark and quality of what takes place in the New Testament lies in the fact that what was awaited and promised is now being fulfilled. The most striking evidence of this situation is in Romans 3, 21: "But now the righteousness of God has been manifested apart from law," and in the emphasis of the captivity epistles—that what was previously a hidden mystery has now been revealed (Colossians 1, 26; Ephesians 3, 5). The famous opening of the Epistle to the Hebrews ex-

72

plicitly emphasizes this aspect: "In many and various ways God spoke of old to our fathers by the prophets; but in these last days he has spoken to us by a Son." In present-day theology the concept "eschatological" has come to mean the time revealed in Jesus Christ as the final phase of time. This present moment is fulfilled in such a way that it is possible to speak of the fullness (*pleroma*) of time (Galatians 4, 4). It cannot be surpassed by anything in the future, and the whole future is a future which consists of this present moment.

If we consider these facts and circumstances, we find that Rudolf Bultmann's theology and his understanding of revelation —which convincingly emphasize the present, the *now* and *today* of the Christ event that again specifically qualifies the lasting presence through the *now* of proclamation—gets at the kernel of the New Testament revelation, of revelation as fulfillment in the sense of the now, the today, the ultimate. But Bultmann allows no place for any real future which is still awaited; he makes everything belong to an eschatology in the decisive event taking place at the present time. All future echatology is a myth which must be demythologized into its present and existential meaning. His position is radical, one-sided in a way which does not do justice to the full testimony of the New Testament (precisely in its definition of time). But the theological conception of Bultmann is more in accordance with the significance of the event of revelation to which the New Testament bears witness, than are theological theories which attempt to place the Old and the New Testaments on the same level, failing to express the "now" of the New Testament, the "fullness of time" to which the New Testament bears witness, and the *kairos* which is fulfilled. Other theories which make the expectation of the future the heart of the New Testament revelation fail to do justice to the fulfillment which it contains.

73

b. The Fulfillment of Revelation: "Behold!"

One can also describe the phenomenon of revelation as fulfillment in terms of the immediate presence characterized by the
demonstrative "Behold!" In the concrete presence of a person,
Jesus of Nazareth, and in the presence of his life, word, work,
happening, and destiny, revelation attained a fulfillment beyond which nothing more can be expected. The Bible describes
the distinctive quality of the immediate presence in which
revelation was fulfilled in the person and the work of Jesus
Christ in several ways, and the New Testament makes use of
a number of different categories for this purpose.

For example, Jesus is called rabbi, the *teacher*, but Jesus is
spoken of as a teacher in an unmistakably emphatic way:
"What is this? A new teaching! With *authority* . . ." (Mark
1, 27). "You have *one* teacher, and you are all brethren"
(Matthew 23, 8). This sets him off from other teachers. The
distinction is made even greater by the fact that it is not the
disciples who seek the rabbi, but Jesus who calls them to be
disciples. With Jesus the disciple can never be or become
a master himself. As a teacher, Jesus (in a fundamentally different way from such a teacher as Buddha) does not hide
behind his doctrine, but is one with what he says—the message
he proclaims is really and ultimately himself. This process is
consummated within the history to which the New Testament
bears witness. Jesus, who proclaims himself, becomes Christ
who is proclaimed—this is the content of every message,
preaching, and proclamation of Jesus Christ. All nations are
to become his disciples (Matthew 28, 19).

The New Testament also calls Jesus the *prophet* (John 1,
21; see also Mark 6, 4), meaning by this the long expected, final,
and ultimate prophet who is to be the consummation of all
prophecy at the end of time. He brings revelation in the same

way as God had given it in the law of Moses. His call to re-
pentance is seen as the ultimate eschatological commandment
of God. Whereas the New Testament emphasizes that Jesus is
a unique prophet, by asserting that he is the prophet—in an
ultimate and exclusive sense—this attribute is still not an adequate description of the mystery of Jesus. Jesus contrasted
himself with all prophets, even John the Baptist (Matthew 11,
12). "Something greater than Jonah is here" (Matthew 12,
41). The meaning of this is that the event which took place in
Jesus of Nazareth is not merely something relatively greater
than what was to be found in the Old Testament; it refers to
the single, unique person who is "more than a prophet." Brunner draws attention to the fact that no liberal theology has
succeeded in saying what it understands by "more than a
prophet."

Jesus is more than a prophet, because he underwent neither
the calling nor the conversion, neither the crisis nor the resig-
nation, which are characteristic of the figure and career of the
prophet in the Old Testament. Jesus is more than a prophet,
for his mission transcends his human dimension. Jesus is identical with his mission. In contrast to the prophets, Jesus no
longer says, "Thus says the Lord," but: "I say to you"; "I
will it. Be clean"; "I have come"; "I send you"; "I say to you,
arise"; "Lazarus, come out"; "Your sins are forgiven." The
forgiveness of sins and the raising of the dead (as well as
judgment) are the exclusive privilege of God himself, a
privilege which according to the general conception of the Old
Testament is never accorded to his representative, not even to
the Messiah.

The biblical words "more than" are further defined by
Jesus' claim to be more than Solomon (Matthew 12, 42), more
than Moses, the greatest messenger of God in the Old Testament. Jesus places himself above Moses, supersedes the law of
Moses through the authority he claims for himself: "You have

heard that it was said to the men of old . . . But I say to you" (Matthew 5, 21 ff.). This authority made the law so radical that it extended even to the intention of the heart, and at the same time simplified and intensified it, by defining it as the expression of the holiness of God, the holy will of God.

The extent to which Jesus regarded himself as fulfillment is shown by his radical call to follow him. This includes a readiness to allow nothing and no one to be a hindrance, if necessary to renounce everything, to share in the life and destiny of Jesus including the "cross."

The imitation of Jesus becomes the new principle of moral action: Paul raises it to the level of a demand: "Have this mind among yourselves, which you have in Christ Jesus" (Philippians 2, 5). The most impressive fulfillment lies in the fact that Jesus became the standard of human action, and in fact is the measure by which the final judgment is made (Matthew 25, 40). So it is understandable that Jesus demands the acknowledgement of his person, for our final salvation or damnation is decided by our attitude to Jesus: "Everyone who acknowledges me before men, I also will acknowledge before my Father who is in heaven; but whoever denies me before men, I also will deny before my Father who is in heaven" (Matthew 10, 32 f.; see Luke 12, 7; Mark 8, 38).

All these assertions express the way in which the immediate presence of revelation in Jesus of Nazareth transcends and is "more than" what preceded it, and is therefore the fulfillment of revelation. *The person of Jesus stands in the place of God.* The authority of the prophetic word is transferred to a person who is present here and now, the fulfillment of revelation which took place in and through Jesus. The mystery of divine authority in a person is the mystery of Jesus and his revelation. The authority of Jesus is the authority of God himself. When Jesus speaks, God himself speaks; when he acts, God acts; in his personal presence, the personal presence of God has come about as a fact.

Finally, revelation as fulfillment is given in the fact that Jesus, unlike the prophets and John the Baptist, does not merely proclaim the message of the kingdom and rule of God, but makes this theme the central point of his own preaching. He frees the conception of the kingdom of God from all contemporary, earthly, political, and national misunderstandings. Raised to a religious and universal level, the βασιλεία is the gracious condescencion of God, the power of God against the rule of evil, sin, and death, as grace, peace, and "eternal" life, and as the salvation of man. God's kingdom is an exclusive gift for which man prays (see Matthew 6, 10). In his preaching, Jesus announces the direct and imminent presence of the kingdom of God (Mark 1, 15), and defines the "condition of entry" into the kingdom of God. These include *metanoia* as the abandonment of all human autonomy and as the recognition that God is Lord, together with a readiness to deny oneself, to become like a child, to imitate Jesus himself.

God is present in Jesus. Jesus' actions are an impressive confirmation of this fact. As mighty acts (δυνάμεις) of a kind which are reserved to God, they are not only the fulfillment of messianic prophecies, as Jesus says in his answer to the question put by John the Baptist (see Matthew 11, 4–11), they are signs of the kingdom of God inaugurated in him, and in which sickness, death, and sin are overcome. "But if it is by the finger of God that I cast out demons, then the kingdom of God has come upon you" (Luke 11, 20; Matthew 12, 28). Jesus' power to forgive sins (see Matthew 1–9) is even more impressive than his healings, and is a sign that "the kingdom of God is in the midst of you" (Luke 17, 20). It is clear that what took place in the word and work of Jesus is distinct from the period which extended up to John the Baptist: "The law and the

77

prophets were until John; since then the good news of the kingdom of God is preached" (Luke 16, 16).

Origen says that the kingdom and rule of God are the αὐτοβασιλεία of Jesus; he expresses Jesus' kingdom as God's. In the preaching after the resurrection the proclamation of the kingdom of God takes second place to that of Jesus as Christ and Lord. There is a transition from the teaching of Jesus about himself to the preaching of Christ. This, however, does not represent any breach, but is the result of a transition brought about by the death, resurrection, and exaltation of Jesus—a new situation, a transition which implies and assumes a continuity. Clearly, the kingdom and rule of God is present and effective in Jesus Christ.

The unique fulfillment of revelation in its immediate presence in Jesus of Nazareth is also expressed within the New Testament through the description of the unique way in which Jesus is the Son of his Father. In this context, mention must first be made of the "Johannine climax" to the synoptic gospels (Matthew 11, 27): "All things have been delivered to me by my Father; and no one knows the Son except the Father, and no one knows the Father except the Son and anyone to whom the Son chooses to reveal him." Here "Jesus claims to possess a knowledge of God which is wholly similar to the knowledge which the Father possesses of him, and is therefore divine in nature and consequently assumes that his being is divine. All the knowledge of God which men can possess, even that of the prophets, is ignorance by comparison with that which Jesus claims to possess. The reason for this is that he, and he only, is the Son." The Gospel of John itself describes fully and profoundly the exclusive and unique way in which Jesus is the Son: he is the Son as the "only-begotten of the Father," who is therefore the only one—"no one has ever seen God" (John 1, 18)—to bring the revelation of the Father. Jesus is therefore the revealer of God in *person.*

The way in which Jesus is the Son is presented in the Gospel of John as a unique fellowship of knowledge, love, life, and activity with the Father. Jesus does what he sees the Father doing (John 5, 19); he performs the same work as the Father (5, 21–22). "For as the Father has life in himself, so he has granted the Son also to have life in himself" (5, 26). Jesus brings true and ultimate knowledge of God—which at the same time signifies complete fellowship of life with him, "eternal life" (17, 3)—because he knows the Father, "who has sent him," from whom he has come, and who bears testimony to him in works which no one else can do (15, 24). Jesus speaks of what he has heard and seen (3, 11. 28; 8, 26. 28). The Father is in him and he is in the Father (14, 10 f.); he and the Father are one (10, 30). "All that the Father has is mine" (16, 15). Therefore, Jesus claims: "He who hates me hates my Father also" (15, 23), and "He who believes in me, believes not in me but in him who sent me" (12, 44).

The Gospel of John describes the fulfillment given in Jesus in the sense of its immediate presence in him in yet another way, with the characteristic formula "I am." Jesus says: I am the shepherd, the door, the light, the bread, the resurrection, the way, the truth, the life. These expressions assert Jesus' absolute, exclusive, and unique claim, which is further reinforced by such statements as "All who came before me are thieves and robbers" (10, 8); "I am at the door; if anyone enters by me, he will be saved" (10, 9); "No one comes to the Father but by me" (14, 6). The climax of these "I am" sayings is generally accepted to be the use of ἐγώ εἰμι in an absolute sense: "You will die . . . unless you believe that I am he" (8, 24).

This immediate presence of revelation in the sense of Jesus' statement "I am" is the message of the New Testament, and is what distinguishes it from the Old. In Jesus of Nazareth God's self-revelation happened and took shape in an ultimate and unsurpassable way. It is revelation in the form of a person. In Jesus the invisible God disclosed and imparted himself.

c. The Fulfillment of the Categories and Content of Revelation

Fulfillment as a characteristic of the revelation given in Jesus of Nazareth is also expressed by saying that Jesus fulfilled the structures and categories and revelation from the Old Testament: God's word, action, name, and face. The word of Jesus is simply the word of God. That is why "the Word" and "the Word of God" can be used as a title of Jesus Christ (John 1, 14; Revelation 19, 13). In him one can "hear," "see," and "touch," the Word of God (1 John 1, 1). Consequently, in the Incarnate Word—as Heinrich Schlier has said—"the nature of the Word of God, which was already at work in the word of prophecy and of the promise of God to Israel, has been manifested to us completely and ultimately in history. In this Word God has uttered his word—which means himself—in the world."

According to the Old Testament, the word of God is associated with God's action; it is an active word, an historical word, a word which brings about what it utters. In Jesus Christ the word of God and the action of God are united in the Christ event. In the life and activity of Jesus, in his miracles which manifested the power and rule of God, and in what he underwent, especially the cross and the resurrection, his exaltation and the sending of the Spirit, there took place the ultimate act of God, which happened once, and at the same time once for all, transforming everything and making it new.

The same is true of the category of the name of God. In Jesus the name "which is above every name" (Philippians, 2, 9) is given. The name of Jesus manifests ultimately and finally what was meant by the name of God from the very first, but

80

was never completely fulfilled in a real sense: God himself, as a present and personal reality, as a mystery disclosed and made known. In the name of Jesus men have the name through which all are saved (Acts 4, 12). In this name we call on God, and God hears. "If you ask anything of the Father, he will give it to you in my name" (John 16, 23).

Again, the same is true of the category of the face of the Lord. This is an expression of the divine grace and mercy, and of direct access to it. This category, as we have shown above, casts a particularly revealing light on the character of the Old Testament as promise. The face that is sought is nowhere truly present. In the New Testament this category is fulfilled, for "It is the God who said, 'Let light shine out of darkness,' who has shone in our hearts to give the light of the knowledge of the glory of God in the face of Christ" (2 Corinthians 4, 6). The glory of God has shone in the face of Jesus Christ, not as a reflection as in the case of Moses, but as the splendor of God himself. Πρόσωπον, the word used here, means both face and person. The face of God is the face of a person: the Incarnate Word, whose glory (δόξα) was to be seen upon earth (John 1, 14). Thus Jesus says in the Gospel of John: "He who has seen me has seen the Father" (14, 9). Christ is the epiphany of God. Consequently, Christ is also the image, the *eikon* of the invisible God (2 Corinthians 4, 4; Colossians 1, 15), infinitely more than man can be the image and likeness of God. In its New Testament meaning, "image" is identical with glory and signifies the person present in the image. Thus this statement is also a confession of the exclusive personal presence of God in Christ.

Faith in Jesus Christ contains in it the element of hearing and of seeing. The potentiality of human intellectual perception is thereby brought to fulfillment in its totality and it is included in the demand of faith. For this reason, Hans Urs von

81

Balthasar has no qualms about speaking of the "manifest evidence of Christ."

The fulfillment of revelation which took place in Jesus Christ is also found and expressed in the fact (here we turn to the various subjects of revelation) that Jesus is the founder of the new and eternal covenant. The numerous covenants that exist, their constant renewal, and the numerous instruments through which the covenants are mediated are impressive evidence that the Old Testament looked forward to, but never attained, the ultimate covenant. In Christ, as is shown above all by the Last Supper and the self-abandonment of Jesus even to death which took place in it, the new and eternal covenant is concluded and the new, ultimate human religious society is founded (see Matthew 26, 26 f.; Luke 22, 19 f.).

That this covenant is the ultimate covenant is due to the fact (this is the particular theme of the Epistle to the Hebrews) that Jesus Christ, the mediator of the new covenant, is the *Son*, and therefore transcends all other mediators. He supersedes the Old Testament priesthood and the worship of the old covenant, for he is both high priest and sacrifice in one. Because he has offered himself, because he is without sin, because he has no need to offer sacrifice for his own guilt, as a sign of the acceptance of this sacrifice of his he is "exalted above the heavens," and his sacrifice does not merely effect cultic purification, but the forgiveness of sins (Hebrews 4, 14; 5, 1–9; 7, 24. 28; 8–10). The Old Testament was concentrated, and culminated, in the expectation of him who was to come, the anointed, the Messiah. Everything we have said so far is meant to be an answer to the question, "Are you he who is to come, or shall we look for another?" (Matthew 11, 3). Jesus himself answered this question in the affirmative, referring to his fulfillment of the promises to Israel (Matthew 11, 4 ff.). This aim is common to all the gospels, and each seeks to achieve it, in its own way. Most explicit is Matthew, who places all the events surrounding Jesus in the category of the fulfillment of a messianic promise: "This happened, that the Scripture might be fulfilled." The Gospel of John originally closed with the words, "These [signs] are written that you may believe that Jesus is the Christ, the Son of God, and that believing you may have life in his name" (20, 31). Consequently, the confession that Jesus is the Christ is at the heart of Christian faith, prayer, and praise from the very first, and was a legitimate presentation of the message, claim, and life of Jesus.

Jesus Christ is revelation as fulfillment, salvation history which was given at its peak. Christ is the fulfillment of the revelation in the creation of the world and man.

According to Paul, Christ is the "first-born of all creation" (Colossians 1, 15). He is the basis and the goal of creation. For him, creation exists. He who came in the fullness of time is simultaneously he who existed from the first and before all time. This gives a clear picture of the structure and entelechy of the economy of salvation and the history of salvation, the goal of the eternal decrees of the will of God, the mystery of the ages. God "has made known to us in all wisdom and insight the mystery of his will, according to his purpose which he set forth in Christ as a plan for the fullness of time, to unite all things in him, things in heaven and things on earth" (Ephesians 1, 9 f.).

The impressive and powerful theology of this plan is found in John and in the captivity epistles. "In the beginning" in the prologue to the Gospel of John (1, 1) forms a parallel to "in the beginning" in Genesis 1, 1. According to John, the word which was in the beginning and through which everything was made comes from Jesus. He comes as the light which enlightens every man; he comes into the world, which is his own property; and he comes to men, who are his own. A hymn in

83

the Epistle to the Colossians emphasizes the "cosmic status" of Christ: ". . . in him all things were created, in heaven and on earth, visible and invisible, . . . all things were created through him and for him. He is before all things, and in him all things hold together" (1, 16 f.). These ideas are also present in the opening of the Epistle to the Hebrews: "He [the Son] reflects the glory of God and bears the very stamp of his nature, upholding the universe by his word of power" (1, 3). Consequently, Christ is the head of the *cosmos* and of the universe. Thus he can also be called the first and the last, the beginning and the end, the Alpha and Omega (Revelation 1, 17; 22, 13).

If Christ is not merely the basis but also the goal of creation, then the aspect of creation as revelation is once again clearly manifested. *Creation is planned for Christ.* Christ is the consummation of the creation, the final word of the words of creation, the highest fulfillment and consummation of all the works of creation, especially man, who has found in Christ his new and proper image. Jesus is the true man, the second and real Adam (see 1 Corinthians 15, 21 f. 45–49). The image provided by this man is grounded in God, infinitely open to God, a hearer of his word, obediently fulfilling his will, loving God above everything, and consequently closely bound to men in selfless devotion and brotherly service. This image of man expresses the fundamental law of human nature: the closer a man is to God, the closer he is to himself.

Jesus is Christ, the Messiah; this title proclaims the fact that Jesus is the fulfillment of the promise and revelation. The title of Lord proclaims in what way Jesus is the Christ. However, the confession that Jesus is the *Kyrios* also means that he is the fulfillment of the revelation from man and creation. *Kyrios* is a translation of God's Old Testament name Yahweh; Jesus is Lord because as the bodily and personal presence of God, he is the instrument of the kingly rule of God. The primitive Christian creed and the substance of primitive Christian faith is summed up in the words: Jesus Christ, *Kyrios*, Jesus is the Christ, Jesus is Lord (Philippians 2, 11).

The ultimate act of revelation in the person and life of Jesus, according to the New Testament the most convincing proof that Jesus is Christ and *Kyrios*, is the rising of Jesus from the dead. "Let all the house of Israel therefore know assuredly that God has made him both Lord and Christ, this Jesus whom you crucified" (Acts 2, 36). Through the resurrection from the dead God has "given assurance" of Jesus "to all men" (Acts 17, 21). This is why the resurrection of Jesus is the *content* and *basis* of Christian preaching and of faith. "If Christ has not been raised," Paul explains, "then our preaching is in vain and your faith is in vain" (1 Corinthians 15, 14). "But in fact Christ has been raised from the dead, the first fruits of those who have fallen asleep" (1 Corinthians 15, 20). Paul can sum up the content of Christian faith in these words: "If you confess with your lips that Jesus is Lord and believe in your heart that God raised him from the dead, you will be saved" (Romans 10, 9).

Günther Bornkamm says that "it is certain in a wholly historical sense" that "there would be no gospel, no single New Testament story, no New Testament epistles, no faith, no Church, no worship, and no prayer in Christianity up to the present day without the gospel of the resurrection of Jesus." The obvious fact that it is not the event of the resurrection itself, but only faith in the resurrection and the preaching of it which are historically verifiable must be complemented by the equally obvious fact that the exclusive content of this faith and this preaching is based upon the event of the resurrection. The accounts of the resurrection display significant differences in details; they all converge upon the idubitable fact of the resurrection. The "witnesses of the resurrection" testify to the resurrection through their encounter with him who is now "truly" risen, although he was crucified and lay in the grave.

The question much discussed in present-day theology, whether the resurrection of Jesus was an historical fact or not, depends upon what one means by an historical fact. If the characteristic of an historical fact is that it can be explained by its natural processes, that the course of what happened in it can be observed, and that it displays analogies with other historical events, then the resurrection of Jesus is not an historical fact, for it fulfills none of these conditions. As an event and as a mode of existence, the resurrection of Jesus is something completely new, totally different from everything else that occurs historically and empirically. It is the inauguration of the new and final aeon, which is not characterized by the fact "that a dead man has come back to life," but by the fact that death is finally conquered. As Walter Künneth puts it, the resurrection has only one meaningful parallel: the creation of the world.

It therefore follows that the resurrection as an event, an occurrence, and a fact transcends historical factuality; but though it was an occurrence without empirical causality or analogy, it nevertheless took place within the world and historical time, as a reality "not of this world, but an entrance into this world." It is possible to apply the term "historical fact" to such a possibility and reality within history. For history is the realm of what is new and unexpected, the realm of freedom, the realm where God's freedom and sovereignty can be exercised. In this sense the resurrection of Jesus is an historical fact in the preëminent sense of the word.

The resurrection of Jesus shows that Jesus as Christ and Lord is revelation's fulfillment. Meditating on this idea, Paul says, "The Son of God, Jesus Christ, whom we preached among you, . . . was not Yes and No; but in him it is always Yes. For all the promises of God find their Yes in him. That is why we utter the Amen through him, to the glory of God" (2 Corinthians 1, 19 f.).

86

Our account of the fulfillment of revelation in Jesus Christ would be incomplete if it did not take into account the saving work of Jesus after he was risen from the dead and exalted: the sending of the Spirit. As the Spirit of God in the Old Testament, the Spirit was described as the life-giving and effective power of God experienced in history and the creation. It is said of him that he spoke by the prophets (Hebrews 1, 1). The prophets attributed this Spirit to "him who was to come" to a special degree (Isaiah 42, 1–3; 61, 1 f.); the coming of the Spirit was regarded as the promise of eschatological consummation (see Joel 3, 1–5; Zechariah 12, 10). The Holy Spirit was at work in the earthly origin (Luke 1, 35), the life, the word, and the acts of Jesus (see Mark 12, 28; Luke 11, 20). The presence of this Spirit, the "Spirit of the Lord," was claimed by Jesus in a special way (Luke 4, 18), and revealed in him in his "messianic consecration" (Matthew 3, 16; Mark 1, 8).

According to the Gospel of John this Spirit was promised by Jesus to his followers as the ἄλλος παράκλητος, "another counsellor," to assist and help them. Following on his promise, the explicit statement is made that the Paraclete would only come after Jesus had been glorified (7, 39), and had gone to the Father (16, 9). It is said of the Paraclete that he is the "Spirit of truth" who will be with Jesus' followers for ever (14, 6 f.). His work is described in the following words: "He will teach you all things, and bring to your remembrance all that I have said to you" (14, 26); "He will bear witness to me" (15, 26); "He will guide you into all the truth" (16, 13); "He will glorify me, for he will take what is mine and declare it to you" (16, 14); he will "convince" the world that there is sin, righteousness, and judgment (16, 8).

This promise of the coming of the Spirit (Acts 1, 8) was fulfilled at Pentecost (Acts 2). This event sealed revelation fulfilled in Christ. For through the Spirit, the Spirit of Christ and the Spirit of the Father, through his rule and activity a permanent continuation, perpetual presence, accessibility, and appropriation of salvation brought for all men by Christ were given.

Paul describes the profound way in which the "Spirit of the Lord," the "Spirit of Christ," the "Holy Spirit," is the essence of Christian existential life. He describes this life either as "being in Christ" or as "living in the Spirit." In the Holy Spirit the mystery of Christ is known (1 Corinthians 12, 3) together with the new existence of believers, who know that they are "sons of God" (Galatians 4, 5) and can cry "Abba! Father!" (Romans 8, 15). We have access to the Father through Christ in one Spirit (Ephesians 2, 18). The Church, for Paul, is the body of Christ whether in the individual congregation or the Church encompassing all "churches." It is inspired, in its variety of persons, offices, and gifts, by the one Spirit and built up into a unity (1 Corinthians 12; see also Ephesians 4, 4). To this extent, it is right and justifiable to speak of the Church as the "continuation of the anointing of Jesus with the Holy Spirit" in salvation history, or as the mystery of the identity of the Holy Spirit in Christ and in Christians.

The Holy Spirit assures and actualizes the saving work of Christ. This takes place in the word of the apostolic preaching, through which the Spirit remains the truth. It becomes the kerygma of Jesus, Christ and Lord.

The saving tasks are committed to those who were chosen and called by the historic Jesus, first of all as the "twelve." Jesus gives them a share in his own messianic task (Mark 3, 14–17); he allows them to represent him (Luke 10, 16): "He who hears you hears me, and he who rejects you rejects me." The "eleven"—in the new, apostolic situation—become witnesses of the resurrection and of the risen Jesus, and the risen

Jesus once again sends them forth: "As the Father has sent me, even so I send you" (John 20, 21). From the risen Christ they receive a universal task: "All authority in heaven and on earth has been given to me. Go therefore and make disciples of all nations, baptizing them in the name of the Father and of the Son and of the Holy Spirit, teaching them to observe all that I have commanded you; and lo, I am with you always, to the close of the age" (Matthew 28, 18–20). They are given power and ability to carry out this task through receiving the fullness of the Spirit of Christ; they become *apostles*, messengers and witnesses of Jesus Christ. The Church, which itself went forth into the world at Pentecost, is built on the foundation of the apostles and prophets (Ephesians 20, 2), and so becomes an Apostolic Church.

Two things are clear about the apostle and his function which are important for a theology of revelation. First, the apostles and their office, and especially their preaching of Jesus as Christ and Lord, are part of the event, occurrence, and work of revelation fulfilled in Jesus Christ. It is Jesus Christ who has set them this task. The apostle "stands within the process of revelation." He is "himself the recipient of revelation and the witness of revelation, and therefore, together with Christ the original author, is the source of a tradition of which those who follow the apostles are the first to become merely vehicles and witnesses. . . . The apostles, who received the revelation of God in Jesus Christ crucified and exalted, and were called and sent forth as his witnesses, form part of that revelation. . . . The apostles are with Christ in a unique and unrepeatable way; and Christ, by his own will, is not present without the apostles."

Secondly, the implicit and necessary consequence of this fact is that the revelation brought to fulfillment in Jesus Christ is "concluded with the apostles." Of course, it is impossible to determine when this conclusion occurred in terms of an

89

exact date, but we can grasp what it means. It includes the
fundamental distinction between revelation and tradition,
origin and succession, the source and the stream, the con-
stitutive norm and the continuation, the standard and what is
based upon that standard. This expresses once again the fact
that revelation fulfilled in Jesus Christ and in his works was
given once and for all and cannot be superseded; there is no
radically new source of revelation in the sense of the personal
self-manifestation of God. We have a continuing tradition,
but a tradition in and from its origin, an unfolding development. This brings apprehension and understanding to the
"original fullness" in all its breadth and depth. The future is
the future of this revelation fulfilled in Jesus Christ.

The God of Israel to whom the Old Testament bears witness, the one and only Lord, reveals himself in the revelation
of the New Testament as the God who manifests himself
through his Son in the Holy Spirit. This revelation is definitive,
ultimate, and eschatological. Revelation in the form of a promise took place in the course of a particular people's history,
although it was a sign to all nations. Revelation as fulfillment
is exclusive, insofar as it is concentrated upon a single person
and upon what took place in that person: Jesus and the Christ
event. This exclusiveness, however, is linked with a universality to which there are no longer any limits: the salvation
manifested by the Father through the Son in the Holy Spirit
is salvation for all men, for all humanity.

The new Israel is the Church, and because of its universal
mission, it is necessarily a universal Church, a Church for all
humanity, the people of God drawn from among the peoples
of the earth. The Church, humanity, and world are, naturally,
not identical. But it is the mission and task of the Church to
bear witness to and to present in historical, concrete, existential
form the fact that the all-inclusive gracious will of God is

present in Jesus Christ as salvation for the whole of mankind, offered to all men. In this way, the Church and mankind (which "share the humanity of Jesus Christ"), like general and the special history of salvation, are coordinated with one another. The Church has a task of salvation to carry out for the whole world; the Church exists not for its own glorification, but for others; it is a sign of the merciful love of God towards all men. This service carried out for the whole world would not exist, however, without a Church. So the Church does have a task "of glorifying God through its whole existential being, and of extolling the grace of God offered to the whole of sinful mankind in Christ, in behalf of everyone." The Church possesses a *representative* function, a function to which theology must pay particular attention, today. "In order that it can be the salvation of all men, the Church does not have to be identical, even outwardly, with the whole of mankind; its nature consists rather in this, that in the imitation of Christ, who was the One, it represents the few through whom God will save the many. Its task is not carried out by all, but is done in behalf of all."

Revelation as promise is in history. In the same way, history possesses revelation in Christ so that it took place once, "once for all," and so cannot be repeated in history. Yet it makes possible a real history, insofar as it is a turning point in history and discloses the new way as God's definitive revelation is brought to full maturity in all its dimensions. This new way is at the same time the beginning of the return of the world to the Father, in which it repeats the way followed by Christ: "I come from the Father and have come into the world; again, I am leaving the world and going to the Father" (John 16, 28).

The attempt has been made to define the relationship between the old and the new covenants in terms of the law and

91

the gospel, the law and grace, the law and freedom. A one-sided picture is produced by simply identifying the old covenant with the law, and the new covenant with the gospel of grace and freedom.

The difference is how law and grace are conveyed to man. Augustine defines the difference by describing the former as externally imposed and the latter as an inward gift. He formulates their relationship in the well-known saying: "The law (in the old covenant) was given that the promised grace might be sought; grace (in the new covenant) was given that the law might be fulfilled." Grace manifests the inner relationship between promise and fulfillment; it includes and transforms the concept of the law. Aquinas writes, "The law of the new covenant is the grace of the Holy Spirit given to the faithful." The gospel gives a new form to the law; it brings together the giving of the law and the fulfillment of the law, so that in grace the law of God becomes the gift of God. In Augustine's words, "Give what you command, and command what you will."

In this light it is clear what is meant by saying that Christ is the "end and fulfillment of the law" (Romans 10, 4). The law cannot be the form taken by the gospel; rather, the gospel is the form of the law, its essential structure. The way of those who are called to the revelation of Christ does not lead from the law to grace and freedom—that was the way within revelation as promise—but from freedom and grace to the fulfillment of the law. In Christ's revelation the way no longer leads through works to grace, but through grace to works. In New Testament terms, the works are the fruits of grace, for Paul the "fruits of the Spirit." John describes them Christologically in the image of the vine and the branches: "I am the vine, you are the branches. He who abides in me, and I in him, he it is that bears much fruit, for apart from me you can do nothing" (John 15, 5).

92

4. REVELATION AS COMPLETION

The heart of everything, revelation in Jesus, Christ and Lord, is, also, in a quite definite sense the end and the consummation, the eschatological event. Yet revelation as fulfillment still has a future, its own future which is not yet present but awaited. The future is the consummation of what has already definitively taken place and come about; the future has already begun in the central event. It is rooted and grounded in that event, and can only mean the "bringing to a conclusion" of what has already begun: the removal of what is "not yet" from what "already is."

Still, there is an aspect in revelation which is not yet present, and a consummation which will come about in the future. The primary indication of this fact is given by the eschatological sayings of Jesus, the saying concerning the "coming of the Son of man in great power and glory," and the sayings concerning the judgment, and the new heaven and the new earth. On the one hand, the kingdom of God is proclaimed and brought into being in Jesus Christ. His words and deeds, and especially his resurrection from the dead and the sending of the Spirit, are unmistakable signs of this fact and reality. But at the same time we find a prayer for the coming of this kingdom: "Thy kingdom come," "Maranatha." The parables of the growing seed point towards this future, as do the commands to watch, to wait, to be ready, to be patient, to struggle, to have faith, and to hope. "For in this hope we were saved. Now the hope that is seen is not hope. . . . But if we hope for what we do not see, we wait for it with patience" (Romans 8, 24 f.).

The revelation in Jesus is a revelation in the form of a servant, in loneliness, in the scandal of the cross. This means that regardless of any revelation in the form of authority and

93

sovereignty, it is a concealed revelation and a revelation of the concealment of God. Only faith is capable of overcoming this scandal and tolerating the mixture of manifestation and concealment which revelation in Jesus contains. This fact must be maintained along with the message and fact of the resurrection. But we have access only to the resurrection through the "witnesses of the resurrection." The risen Christ did not appear to the whole world, but only to his chosen witnesses (see Acts 10, 40). Everyone else is to be brought to faith in the risen Christ through their word. While faith is certainly a gift of God, a light upon the way, a foundation, a sustenance, and a certainty, and "the victory that overcomes the world" (1 John 5, 4), it is also the "virtue of those who are on pilgrimage" and points beyond itself to a consummation which the Scripture describes as seeing God "face to face" and as to "understand fully, even as I have been fully understood" (1 Corinthians 13, 12).

The resurrection of Jesus is the beginning of the consummation; it is the assurance and pledge of everything that is to be hoped, Christ is "the hope of glory" (Colossians 1, 27). But the resurrection is only the beginning; its fruits are not yet everywhere effective. The signs of what is opposed to God (sickness, suffering, sin, and death) are still present, creation still groans. We who have already been redeemed wait for the "redemption of our bodies" (Romans 8, 23). The celebration of the acts of salvation in the sacraments, and above all in the Eucharist, "proclaims the Lord's death until he comes" (1 Corinthians 11, 26).

The work of Jesus is continued through the Paraclete; it is made present in the Church. The being and activity of the Church is characterized by its pilgrimage, its growth to fullness, to the full stature of Christ, to the full Christus. The Church is the "wandering people of God."

All these things are signs of what is "not yet." But this

situation cannot last for ever; what is "already" present in what is "not yet" must attain to an unimpaired consummation, and so to the consummation of revelation, in which Christ, the Alpha, will be revealed as the Omega (Revelation 1, 8; 21, 6; 22, 13). "It does not yet appear what we shall be, but we know that when he appears we shall be like him, for we shall see him as he is" (1 John 3, 2). From the point of view of him who reveals, revelation as consummation is "revelation in power and glory," while for men it means to see "face to face," to "understand fully, even as I have been fully understood."

The kingdom of God will be acknowledged by the whole world at the eschaton. The distinction between mankind and the Church will be abolished, and there will be a unity between the new heaven and the new earth (Revelation 21, 1). The Son will hand the kingdom over to the Father, "that God may be everything to everyone" (1 Corinthians 15, 28).

Eschatologically, faith becomes seeing. "To see" implies the removal of the limits imposed upon faith as an indirect form of knowledge. To see is the perfect form of knowledge, direct apprehension and possession. Paul describes seeing as seeing face to face (1 Corinthians 13, 12). The end and consummation restores man to himself—the more one is with God, the more one is truly restored to oneself. This does not result in a featureless abolition of the personality, but is a personal encounter, face to face, and yet a personal encounter combined with the profoundest unity.

What is meant by "to see face to face" is further interpreted by the idea of "knowing, as we are known" (1 Corinthians 13, 12). Knowledge ceases to be fragmentary when God knows in us. This is a way in which God is everything to everyone. Our knowledge is a participation in God's knowledge, a union with the knowledge through which God knows himself. It is the ultimate consummation of "In thy light do we see light"

95

(Psalm 36, 9). But this fact does not remove the distinction between God and man. There is an encounter, a fellowship, and a unity, but not an identity. The person is maintained in this knowledge, not swallowed up and absorbed by the radiant glory of God, but restored to its true and proper self (1, 5). To be wholly with God means to be wholly oneself.

Revelation as consummation is the consummation of the kingdom of God, and is therefore the form of life in which human salvation is consummated, the consummation of "God revealing himself and the eternal decrees of his will."